C000100246

STEALTH MILLIONAIRE

HOW TO SAVE MONEY AND MANAGE YOUR MONEY LIKE THE RICH

GEORGE CHOY & SARAH CHOY

First published in the United Kingdom on 12 May 2020
by My Castle Property Training LLP
11 Abbott Way, Tenterden, Kent, TN30 7BZ, United Kingdom.
mycastleproperty.co.uk

This version 1.4 edition published on 1 May
2021
© 2020 George David Choy & Sarah Jane Choy

British Library Cataloguing in Publication Data
A catalogue record is available for this book

Paperback ISBN: 9798630455772

My Castle Property Training LLP
11 Abbott Way, Tenterden, Kent, TN30 7BZ, United Kingdom.

Disclaimer

This book is intended to provide general information about investing, saving, mortgages, money management, debt management, company incorporation, tax, trusts, leasing and mindset. It is not an advice book, and its contents are not tailored to your specific circumstances. In particular, the contents of this book does not constitute financial advice and neither the authors nor My Castle Property Training LLP are regulated financial advisors.

You must not rely on the information in this book or the accompanying materials available for download as an alternative to financial, investment, legal, taxation, accountancy or advice from an appropriately qualified professional. You should never delay seeking professional advice because of the information contained in this report.

No warranty is made with respect to the accuracy or completeness of the information contained. Both the authors and My Castle Property Training LLP specifically disclaim any responsibility for liability, loss, or risk, personal or otherwise, which is incurred as a consequence, directly or indirectly of the use and application of any of the contents of this book or any accompanying downloads.

This disclaimer will be governed by and construed in accordance with English law, and any disputes relating to this disclaimer will be subject to the exclusive jurisdiction of the courts of England and Wales.

IMAGINE EARNING YOUR FIRST MILLION...

Close your eyes and think about it.

What will you life look like?

What kind of house will you live in?

How will you spend your days with your loved ones?

Which far off countries will you travel to?

But…you're wondering what steps do you need to take to make your new life a reality?

We completely replaced our incomes when Sarah was only 39 years old and have a property portfolio worth £2 million.

We can show you exactly how we did it, by taking you step-by-step through what it takes to become completely Financially Free.

We can help you to create an action plan, and support you carrying it out — so you never need to worry about money again.

To Achieve your Dream Life faster, visit
mycastleproperty.co.uk/training

Dedication

**For our children and their piggy banks
— may they become wise and wealthy.**

Acknowledgements

Thanks to all the Stealth Millionaires we interviewed for this book — Richard Snell, Andrew Bartlett, Joy Savill, and Linda and Brian Carter.

Thanks to Tim Ferris for inspiring us to design our dream lifestyle.

Also, thanks to Mr. Money Mustache for inspiring us to get our ridiculously expensive lifestyle under control, so we could become financially free when Sarah was only 39.

A final thanks to both our parents for making us what we are today.

George & Sarah Choy

Contents

Introduction

We became Millionaires and retired when Sarah was only 39 years old. This was way ahead of all of our friends, who still continue to work, as they need their job to survive.

We weren't born with a silver spoon in our mouths.

We didn't go to private school.

We didn't inherit the money.

We built it ourselves.

We have about £2 million of investment property. We didn't inherit the money to start this. We began with very little cash and grew it ourselves, out of nothing. **So if you have no money like we did, then you can do it too.**

We could have retired in our twenties, if we had learned the key lessons in this book. **The big secret to becoming a Millionaire** is not about being a high-earner.

The secret is being able to hold onto more wealth — something that **even someone on a low income could do**, as you'll see later.

We live in a 4-bedroom detached house with our two children 9 and 10, and our cat. The area is a lovely historic town, with plenty of countryside surrounding it. We are only a ten-minute walk to the shops, and one-minute walk to a forest.

Stealth Millionaires are the millionaires next door. At first glance, they appear to lead regular lives. But they have the financial stability to do whatever they want, whenever they want. **They have the freedom to choose.**

To most people, we appear to be a "normal" upper-middle-class family. However, most of our neighbours are 10-20 years older than us, as the gap between wages and home ownership gets wider every year.

We live close enough to walk our children to and from school. We do our household chores whilst they're there, so we can spend more time with them when they're back.

What makes us different is the freedom we have. How we can choose how we spend our time.

I bet you're wondering…what do our days look like?

We're up at 5am, before our children rise. This gives Sarah and me some time on our own. At 6am we workout in our home gym — and by the time we finish at 7am, our children are awake. We hang around with them, and then walk them to school.

If we're having an "at home" day, then we do a few business-related tasks in our home office. We check our bank accounts and revenue. We take care of any household tasks — chores you save up for the weekend…we do during the week.

After that, we typically spend the afternoon in the garden, reading a book, or listening to podcasts.

On the other hand, Sarah and I often have a day out while our children are at school. We like to spend a relaxing day at a spa, having a massage…or a vineyard tour, visiting a theme park.

We both love movies. So, one great benefits of going to the movies during the day is that you get a private cinema. We're the only ones there! We can sit exactly where we want.

I once posted on Facebook that I was on a brewery tour, and currently tasting a selection of beers. My friend Emma texted me back to ask whether I was having a Christmas party (as she was booked into one on the same day). I replied that it was "just a normal weekday for us — nothing unusual!" And before you ask…our children's grandmother would be picking up our kids from school.

We usually don't tell our children what we've been up to — so they just assume we've been sitting at home all day.

One day I heard my daughter screaming "Nooooo" when she discovered a video of us at a theme park without her! Note to self — remember not to post it to Facebook in future…

We don't have any need for power-dressing suits, so you will always see us walking around in gym clothes, or jeans and a t-shirt. You wouldn't suspect that we are Millionaires.

When we go to the hairdressers, or are shopping during the day, people automatically assume we have the day off from work or are working from home. If they ask us what we do for a living, they are always surprised when we tell them that **every day is a holiday**, as we don't need to work anymore.

Only the wealthy seem to realise that time is more valuable than money. You can't make more.

That's the true meaning of Financial Freedom. **Money is just a tool to make that happen.** To be able to **do what you want...whenever you want.**

Being Financially Free has been a cause of embarrassment for our 10-year-old daughter. One day she told us that the whole class had been asked to say what their parents did for a living.

My daughter felt too ashamed to tell them that we didn't work. In fact, she wanted us to go and get a job! No thanks! One day she will understand.

Let's make one thing clear. **We weren't born Millionaires.**

I had a period when **I was in bad debt** and it kept increasing every month. Sarah and I have had times when **we could barely afford to eat.**

I'm a reformed shopaholic who had poor money-management skills. If I can change, so can you.

We've worked in a number of different occupations over the years, and many of them sucked!

Our jobs have included factory worker, cleaner, child-minder, hospital porter, lab technician, real estate agent, personal trainer, nutritionist, graphic designer, business manager and marketing director.

During our journey, we **spent a lot of time researching self-made Millionaires** and Financial Freedom.
A survey by Fidelity Investments found that 86% of millionaires are self-made, it wasn't handed to them.[1]
So, there's hope for all of us.

Throughout this**, we developed a number of habits** over the years that have been key to our achievement. These are **HABITS that ANYONE can easily do,** to change their future.

Over the course of this book you will get to know the habits of some of our Millionaire and Multi-Millionaire friends.

It was interesting that all our **Millionaires thought they were unique with their habits.**

They may be out of the ordinary, but it turns out the **Millionaires all had very similar routines**. And **those habits can be learned.**

All of our Millionaire friends invest in property.
Sure, you could say that because we invest in property, our friends will be biased towards property too.

However, this isn't by chance. According to Graham Scambler, Emeritus Professor of Sociology, UCL, out

---

[1] Fidelity® Millionaire Outlook 2012

of 1,000 people on The Sunday Times Rich List, the top two most common sources of wealth were:[2]

1. Property
2. Finance and Investments

I also watched my father profit from the stock market, which led to his early retirement. So, we consider the top two ways to get wealthy over the long-term are by investing in property, or the stock market, or both.

We will teach you the 7 habits of the Stealth Millionaires over the course of this book. These are so simple that anyone could do them.

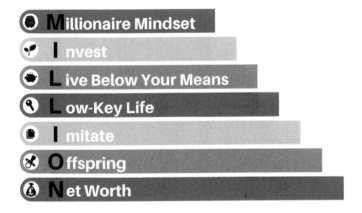

It is within your grasp to create a life where you don't need to worry about money anymore, so you can **live your dreams** and spend time with the people you love.

---

[2] http://www.grahamscambler.com/the-sunday-times-rich-list-2019

Get your mind ready to accept **massive amounts of money. Believe.**

George & Sarah Choy

P.S. If you have any questions you'd like answered while you're reading this book, please post them in our Facebook Group: *Sarah & George Choy Community*

MILLIONAIRE PROFILES:

George Choy & Sarah Choy —Our Story

Our foray into property began with the purchase of our first home together, when Sarah was 21 years old. We bought a tiny — I mean really tiny, stone cottage in the historic village of Limpsfield in Surrey.

It was a one-bedroom house, with a box room big enough for a desk. There was a bus stop outside our window, so we had to make sure we weren't naked with the curtains open, as people on the top deck of the bus could see straight in!

Our first home cost us the princely sum of £97,000, with only £5,000 deposit. We knew we would outgrow it quickly, but it was a start.

We refurbished it and **sold it two years later** for £125,000, making **£28,000 profit**. Little did we know, this would be the start of our property investing adventure.

We next bought something far too big for us, but it needed a lot of work. It was a four-bedroom town house in Westerham, Kent. We paid £164,950.

It hadn't been properly renovated for thirty years, so it was in dire need of a makeover. We redecorated throughout and got it revalued.

The day we became property investors…We discovered we could **pull an extra £68,000 out of our mortgage**, so we did. Did we blow the money on a holiday or car? Nope. We were on a roll…

We didn't think the state pension would be worth much when we retired, and we didn't like the idea of pension money vanishing when one of us died.

Consequently, spurred on by the profit we'd made on our first two houses, we decided to buy a number of investment properties for our retirement — which we assumed, like everyone else, would be at 65 years old.

We'd realised that **splitting our cash into deposits on four cheap houses** would provide us with **better return on our cash**, than only buying one. So we did.

I was working late hours in the City of London and often flying on Sunday, so we didn't have much spare time. We spent our weekends planning which towns to check out and speaking with Estate Agents.

Eventually we decided upon a town and quickly put in offers on four properties, which were accepted. They were **worth a total of £450,000**. **We didn't use any of our own money to buy them**, as all the cash came from re-mortgaging. We still own them today.

Little did we know…**buying four properties at a time turned out to be a total nightmare**! We had four empty properties…four mortgages to pay…no income…and the cost of refurbishments. We were bleeding money!! In hindsight, we should have bought one at a time.

We **spent every weekend decorating** the properties — often working throughout the night. This too was a mistake, as it took us a couple of months to refurbish all four properties on our own — with costs mounting up. In later years we realised our mistake and now pay tradesmen instead. It's faster, and we can be hands off.

We sat back and enjoyed the income from our four free houses, in addition to our day jobs. **The properties contributed towards our lavish lifestyle:** cruises all over the world, our habit of buying designer clothes, and the BMW and Lotus Elise on our driveway.

We knew prices and rents would rise over the long-term, so we just sat back and hoped it would be enough to retire on, when we were elderly.

After three years we decided to move home again. We **sold our town house**, making over **£85,000 profit**. We bought a charming two-bedroom bungalow in Oxted, Surrey, with wooden beams throughout. It was on former farmland, and the farmer used to store and service his tractor in it.

The house was in a poor state, having not been redecorated for thirty years. The kitchen floor was sticky when you trod on it. The whole place needed gutting. We just made it liveable, as we wanted to do a full refurbishment including a loft conversion but couldn't afford to do it as we had stretched ourselves to buy it.

Over the next few years we accumulated enough cash to buy more investment property. **We bought three more over 2 years**, and of course, refurbished them.

With two young children, we eventually saved enough to redevelop our cottage, and put in two extra bedrooms. It was about time…we couldn't keep one of them in a cot in our bedroom for ever.

We rented an apartment nearby, whilst our loft was being developed. I'm so glad we did. The stress was immense, and there was dust everywhere. After three months, the house was finished, and we were now the proud owners of a four-bedroom house in quite an expensive area.

We decided to begin our **quest to research how other people became financially free**. I mean, we had seven investment properties, but we weren't retired yet. What did we need to do? **How had other people become financially free?** The answer to that question is **the seven habits you will learn** in the remainder of this book.

Once we'd learned those habits, **retiring when Sarah was only 39 years old** became a reality. I remember the day so clearly…we worked out our numbers, and Sarah said "Why are we still working? We are already Financially Free!"

So that was it. **We were Millionaires at last**.

We now had freedom. We could do whatever we want, whenever we wanted.

We retired with £1.4 million of investment property at that time.

Since then, our property portfolio has grown to just **over £2 million** and we are involved in £3.8 million of property developments. Our portfolio spans Buy To Let, Rent To Buy and Commercial Property.

We can manage our entire property portfolio in only one hour a month. Now that's work life balance!

We still continue to invest, but our strategy is not to work. We keep everything as passive as possible by outsourcing everything. Time is more valuable to us. If we don't enjoy something, we don't do it. We often work with private investors.

DOWNLOAD FREE RESOURCES TO BUILD YOUR WEALTH
mycastleproperty.co.uk/free-resources

For step-by-step guidance on property investing, see one of our other books:

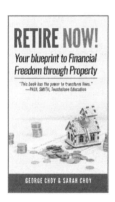

RETIRE NOW! Your Blueprint to Financial Freedom Through Property
mycastleproperty.co.uk/books

Richard Snell — Property Developer

Richard is primarily a Property Developer, working on projects in the millions. He spends his time doing commercial to residential conversions and also new builds.

His investment portfolio of residential, HMO and Serviced Accommodation **amounts to £15 million.**

His parents didn't have a huge amount of money when he was growing up. They taught him to be careful with his spending and not to waste it — particularly food.

As a teenager, he remembers telling people he "wanted to be a millionaire." I bet that teenager wouldn't believe what he's achieved so far!

In his working career, Richard was formerly a manager at British Rail.

Later he left the railways, to become a management consultant at PwC, and bought a property in the City of London. He let out his previous home. That was the start of his property investing career…although he didn't realise that at the time. He viewed himself as an accidental landlord, as it wasn't really planned.

When the dot com bubble burst, Richard lost his job and was given a redundancy package. Richard moved in with his long-term partner, renovated his home and let it out.

After a year off work, he decided he didn't want to go back to that high-pressure life anymore — that was the catalyst for Richard and his partner to become serious property investors.

They bought four flats in west London and leased them to the council for 5-10 years, with guaranteed income.

After that, they went to Edinburgh and bought eight flats and let them all to Edinburgh council. Richard and his partner started off very hands on. Doing it the DIY way took several weeks just to replace a kitchen.

It was a learning experience. Richard has a vivid memory of furnishing three of the flats one evening. They went to Ikea at 9pm and bought all the furniture. He remembers climbing flights of stairs at 1am, carrying a sofa.

Richard said to himself, "we don't want to be doing this again." He has always outsourced the work to other people since then.

By that point he had nine properties in London and eight in Edinburgh - bringing the total to 17 properties.

They scaled up and bought another 40 properties.

Richard feels he has enough residential property now, so his main focus is on developments — where he often works with other investors.

You can contact Richard on Facebook at bit.ly/richardsnell

Andrew Bartlett — Property Developer

Andrew has £5 million of properties under development, £4 million of investment properties and a fully funded SSAS pension. He is a serial property developer.

In his early years, Andrew invested in the stock market with work colleagues in penny shares. They were "a bit speculative" he says, "but we didn't risk thousands". After that he stuck to investing in the government privatised companies such as British Telecom and British Gas.

For 25 years, Andrew also got share options and participated in share save programs when he was employed by Lloyds TSB, including roles such as a Local Director.

At their peak, his bank shares were worth £30,000…but when he came to sell them he only got £1,000. I was telling all my customers "Don't put all your eggs in one basket," and yet I wasn't taking my own advice. So that was a sobering learning.

He wasn't thinking about retiring from his investing at that time — he just used the money to pay for extras like holidays.

For some of his roles at the bank, Andrew often visited property development sites to evaluate them. Some of his colleagues had started buying residential properties and renting them out, but he didn't follow through with it himself.

His investment at that time was in his personal development and career. An unintentional side effect of doing this, was that he got a greater salary, which funded a substantial pension pot.

The turning point for Andrew...

One fortunate day he was on a train from Birmingham and got randomly chatting with one of the passengers. The man's background was in construction. They had a lot of things in common, such as being a similar age, children, and interest in property.

They were both helping other property investors make money — why couldn't they do it too? They decided to have a property business together. Andrew's aim was to provide income for later years...he hadn't considered it could completely replace their income.

They started by converting houses into HMOs — this is where you have multiple people from unrelated households living in the same house. They bought two properties in the first year, four in the second, two in the third year and six in the fourth — just before the housing market crash.

In later years Andrew decided that his investment portfolio was large enough, so he chose not to expand it further, and switched to property development projects.

Throughout his childhood, he helped his mother Barbara Bartlett to raise money to support the church and community. At the age of 81, Barbara was awarded a British Empire Medal in recognition of her lifetime contribution to the community.

That rubbed off on Andrew. He attributed his skills in raising finance and joint venturing in property developments, to his mother.

One pivotal event for Andrew was helping his mother raise finance for extensive repairs to the local Grade I listed medieval church. Needing £25,000 and with only £6 in the church bank account, Barbara had the idea of running a Medieval Weekend. This was so successful, it raised over £15,000.

Consequently, he spends most of his spare time volunteering for the Rotary Club of Malvern, working hands-on, on local community projects or putting on events to raise money to support local causes, such as St Richard's Hospice and Acorns Childrens Hospice.

You can contact Andrew Bartlett on Facebook at bit.ly/andrew-bartlett or see his recent projects at www.stratfordbartlettproperty.com

Joy Savill — Estate Planning Practitioner

Joy primarily works for her company *Stressless Wills*, but also has a passion for property investing. She owns £1.2 million of investment property, plus her home. She invests in Buy To Let, HMO, and land.

This is a far cry from the homeless person she was at 17 years old.

Joy has been working as a conveyancing solicitor for many years. She watched most of her clients getting rich through property investing. Initially she told herself "I do this all day, every day, so I'm not going to do it myself."

The turning point for Joy came when her employment came to an end. She decided to take a year off. She remembers looking at how much her pension was forecast to give her in retirement — it was a shock. It wouldn't even cover a month's rent.

Joy decided to sign up for property training. She purchased two Buy To Let properties within the first six months.

She's bought multiple properties since then, and has a passion for working with charities to house vulnerable young people.

You can contact Joy on Facebook at bit.ly/joysavill

Linda and Brian Carter — Former TV Repair Shop Owners

With Brian at 70 years old, married to Linda, they are the oldest of the Stealth Millionaires. They have £1.4 million in Property and investments.

Linda previously held part-time administration roles in various companies, such as Mazda, and British Telecom. She retired at 55 years old.

Linda recalls that her parents never had much money, when she was growing up. Her dad worked on building sites, and the family just lived from pay cheque to pay cheque. He always worked overtime. They didn't have money, so she was brought up to see money as precious and not to be spent.

The opportunity came for her dad to buy the house they lived in from the council — so he bought it. This was unusual, as at the time, none of his family or friends owned their home. It turned out to be a good investment.

They taught Linda to be careful with her money. Even though Linda didn't have a boyfriend…as soon as she got her first job, she started saving for her first home. She saved a substantial amount, and at 23 years old was able to put down a 30% deposit on a house with Brian.

Brian's spending was more frivolous than Linda's before they got married. He also had the car buying bug that I suffer from and took out loans to pay for them.

In later years, they ran a small TV repair shop and TV rental business. This provided great income for many years, until TVs became cheap and more throwaway.

Their first investment property was a flat in the coastal town of Saltdean, near Brighton. They bought it, renovated it and rented it out to their daughter, who was studying at a university nearby.

When her daughter moved out, Linda and Brian sold it for a very nice profit. Something Linda regrets, as she periodically checked the market value and saw it increase substantially over the years.

The turning point for Linda and Brian was seeing their daughter investing in properties to rent out as Buy To Lets. After watching their daughter build a portfolio — and from the success of their first rental in Saltdean — they decided to do the same.

The rest is history, leading to their early retirement.

CHAPTER ONE:

Net Worth

Track Your Net Worth and Income

Your **Net Worth is the total of all your assets like your house, savings, stocks and shares — minus all your liabilities** such as loans and mortgages. This gives you a single number of what you are worth.

To become a Millionaire, you must aim to grow this figure by acquiring assets.

When I was a Personal Trainer, I found that one of the biggest determinants of losing or maintaining your weight was tracking it. Those people who avoided the scales and never wrote it down, were always doomed to fail.

Our first habit on the path of getting rich was to **write down our Net Worth and Income every month.**

All of the Millionaires tracked this. The majority used an Excel spreadsheet and had kept records for over ten years.

We've done this for many years. It enables us to check that we are still growing and going in the right direction. We prefer to keep track in a spreadsheet, but you can equally write it in notebook. In addition, mortgage providers need to know the value of each of your properties, so you need to know it for refinancing anyway.

Just as people might gain a few pounds and need to diet back to their target weight — our habit also **highlights drops in Net Worth and Income, when you might need a "financial diet"** to get back on track.

Andrew houses students in a number of his HMOs — so, he is able plan his income for up to 18 months from these. He also sets targets for the profit he aims to make every year on commercial to residential conversions.

How Much Are You Actually Spending?

It's a scary experience for most people to actually sit down and work out where all of their wages have gone each month. Most people stick their head in the sand and try to ignore what's happening.

We falsely believed the reason we didn't have any money at the end of each month was because **we didn't earn enough**. It took us a long time to realise how wrong we were…and that even people on very low incomes are able to put aside money for saving each month.

As a first step, **pull out your personal bank and credit card statements** for the last month and arrange your expenditure into categories, so you can **see how much you are spending** on each. Add up the total for the month. It's a scary number — do you feel you got a lot of value out of that hard-earned money?

What usually happens for most people is that they manage to get through the month with their first pay cheque. A couple of years later they get a pay rise and they still don't have any money left at the end of the month.

They've upgraded their lifestyle and are now paying out more per month for their car…membership of a club, fancier holidays, eating at more expensive restaurants and getting a bigger mortgage on another house. Now they have more rooms to fill, and more stuff to buy.

Along comes another pay increase, and they increase their life costs again. Still never having enough money at the end of the month. When they look at the assets they've accumulated, they realise they aren't much wealthier than before.

Looking back at **how you managed to get by on the income from your very first job**, have you managed to save the difference between that and what you earn now — every month?

The answer will be a resounding "no" for 99% of the population. We were caught in that trap.

So, your next step is to **review every single charge** and identify whether you should cancel it, substitute it for a cheaper product or provider, or continue doing it. **Is the**

item really necessary? Make sure to multiply the charges by 12 so you can see the impact per year.

Are you paying too much for your utility bills? Andrew typically reviews these annually and swaps suppliers accordingly.

How about those **coffees you buy every day** on the way to work? You don't notice the cost mounting up, as it's only loose change each day. I was taking someone through this exercise and worked out she spent **£140 a month on coffee**. Did you know **you can lease a small car for less** than that per month!

The smarter move is to **buy a coffee machine** and make your own ground coffee each day and take it with you to work. The machine will pay for itself in 2-3 months.

If you **need help reducing your expenses**, then we recommend you do the **14-Day Money Makeover**. You'll learn ways to find extra money when shopping for groceries, paying your bills, and managing your lifestyle expenses. You'll learn how to make saving a habit and pay off bad debts. **Sign up for this 14-day video series today at mycastleproperty.co.uk/14mm**

When we first did Expense Optimisation for ourselves, we managed to **save £12,000 off our annual expenses**. That is as much as some people earn in a year. So, we gave up our jobs to live off our property income. We were able to quit our jobs in a matter of days! That's how powerful this exercise is.

I helped a friend go through her expenses for a couple of hours and by the end of it **she was £14,600 per year better off.** She saved even more than us!

Frugal Habits Versus Budgeting

If you are spending most of your wages every month, then it could help you to manage your money by setting a **budget** and using what we like to call the **"Pot System".**

You can start the savings habit by **transferring 10% of your monthly earnings into a savings account BEFORE you pay any bills**. Set it up to happen automatically. After a few months, you won't feel the pain of this going out of your wages anymore.

Although saving 10% is low for millionaires. A study of 100 millionaires found that **they typically saved 64% of the income they earned.**[3]

Dr John Demartini takes saving a step further. He recommends people **increase their saving amount by 10% each quarter.** So, by the end of two years the amount you are saving each month will have doubled.

One of my friends, Paul — follows this method and is now putting over £25,000 into savings each month. His savings figure is still increasing every three months.

---

[3] ESI Money, 100 millionaire interviews 2018

However, if you have outstanding **bad debt**, such as pay day loans, or are only making minimum payments on credit card balances, then you should **pay those off before saving.**

It's worth knowing that if you only pay the minimum amount each month, you'll never pay it off. The interest continues to build and keeps you in debt for ever! Aim to pay at least double the minimum payment, if not more.

You could also decide to allocate **10% of your annual wages to education** each year. We spend much more than this, as knowledge helps you to accomplish more, faster.

Perhaps also allocate **10% to charity**. **Be very careful** with charity donations. I've seen people giving a huge proportion of their earnings to charity each month despite being in serious financial difficulties. They want to give, but it will soon make them bankrupt.

Keep it to 10% and use that as the incentive to make even more profit, so you can be more charitable. Be cautious each time you sign up for another charity to automatically debit out of your bank account, as they add up.

And if you're itchy to have some **frivolous spending** money, then **allocate another 10%** to that...and stick to it.

Like all of the Stealth Millionaires...Sarah and I don't budget anymore.

We have a lot of self-control now and **use frugal habits instead**. You can think of it as a code we follow to live our lives.

Every coin or note we earn **is a potential seed for investment.** Every seed grows into more income. Before we open our wallet, we consider whether spending on this provides us with value at that time.

For example, let's take something simple like coffee. We have a ground coffee machine at home, so we have no real need to go to a coffee shop, as it doesn't taste any better. So, if we're wanting one "to go", then we will fill a travel cup with our coffee and take it in the car. No need to go to a drive through.

If we do decide to go to a coffee shop, we think about it in terms of renting meeting space. So, if we are there to brainstorm, have a meeting, or to use their wi-fi for some work, then we are getting value. But we don't ever take away.

If we are travelling for business purposes, such as attending a course, then we mostly stay in clean and functional budget hotels. Something with the standard of a Travelodge or Premier Inn. Most of the millionaires we know, do the same thing.

We spend all day at the conference and then go out for dinner. So, really, we are only using the hotel for sleep and a shower. These are usually a third of the price of the nearby four-star hotels. We usually also bring our own breakfast and decent instant coffee.

The following story sounds like a joke, but it is a true story. The scene is an opulent hotel off the coast of Italy…

Four people go back to the meeting room after their course has finished for that day. I picked up two of the **half-used bottles of water** to take back to my hotel room, as I knew they would get thrown away. Two of the other Millionaires did the same. The fourth person asks why we're doing it, as we have so much money. I answer, **"that's why we are Millionaires."**

The bottled water cost about 10 Euros in the mini bar of our hotel. If there's one gripe I always have about hotels, it's charging for water. Remember, every bank note is a potential seed for investment. The remaining water from the bottle I was drinking at the meeting was no different to the one in the mini bar in my hotel room, so why waste the money.

Another example. When we're taking our kids for a day out at a venue, and I happen to know that the restaurants only serve fast food — if the weather is warm, we always bring a picnic. Better food, at less cost.

I'll only part with the money for something frivolous, if I believe I'm getting good enough value by spending it. Value comes in many shapes and sizes…it's not always about buying the cheapest thing.

Regularly Check Your Bank Balances

We have **multiple bank accounts**. One of our habits is to check our bank balances every day, to make sure we don't go overdrawn and to shuffle money from one account to another as required.

We are not alone in this habit. All the other Millionaires do this too.

The majority of the **Stealth Millionaires checked their bank accounts daily.** Brian likes to leave only £300 in their current account and sweep all the excess immediately into savings every day.

In addition, both Richard and Joy **pay someone to check that the income from rents have been received** on time.

Courage Pot

I first recommended people set up a Courage Pot in one of our books, *RETIRE NOW! Your Blueprint to Financial Freedom Through Property*.

All the Millionaires I spoke to, had one.

We've had many ups and downs over the years. Sometimes we were right on the breadline, barely having enough money to buy food.

Unforeseen circumstances seem to happen every couple of years. We've been through a property crash and recession with our investment properties. We've had half of our rental properties vacant at the same time.

There have been changes in regulations and tax for property investors. We been in complete lockdown during the Coronavirus pandemic.

Black swan events are unpredictable and can have severe consequences.

Whatever happens, the only way to prepare for a black swan is to have investments you can liquidate with short notice, to weather the storm.

What we previously recommended was to hold six months of your business expenses in cash — that's what most of the Stealth Millionaires held.

However, since the Coronavirus pandemic we have increased our **Courage Pot target to one year of business expenses.**

This target assumes that you run your own business, or own assets that require operating expenses such as rental property. **Alternatively hold a year of your personal living expenses in cash — whichever is larger.**

When we add another property to our portfolio, we also add to our Courage Pot at the same time.

Your Courage Pot should be liquid. It could be cash savings, gold, silver, watches, or anything you could turn into cash quickly. Be wary of holding this pot in stocks and shares, as the markets crash very fast when a black swan event happens, so you'll have less money. After the Coronavirus pandemic I wonder whether toilet roll should be added to this list, as it was rarer than gold in the supermarket!

Having this Courage Pot gives you the reassurance of knowing that if the worst happens and you have absolutely no income at all, you can survive. You will have a roof over your head and food to eat. It helps to keep your stress levels down when anything happens.

The other issue we found when we were short of money in the past was making **stupid decisions and acting desperate.** People can smell the fear on you, and they don't want to have anything to do with you.

Your courage pot will keep you sane!

Chapter One Summary:
Net Worth
- Check your bank balances every day
- Track your Net Worth and Income every month
- Monitor your personal expenses at least once a month
- Analyse where you are currently spending your money and reduce it
- Develop frugal habits and stop wasting money on things you don't really need
- Set aside a liquid *Courage Pot* with 6-12 months of your personal or business expenses in it (whichever is bigger)

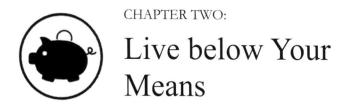

CHAPTER TWO:

Live below Your Means

All of the Stealth Millionaires lived below their means — **they didn't spend more than they earned.**

This wasn't always the case, as the majority had experienced some bad debt on credit cards in their earlier lives. They learned from this not to do it again.

Linda was the only person who had always lived below her means. When she was on very low wages early in life, she just didn't go out, or spend on anything frivolous.

That's very different from most people, who are up to their eyeballs in car finance, furniture finance and credit card debt.

Joy's homelessness taught her to be careful with money. She has a habit of squeezing every last drop out of toiletries…and everything she's paid for.

"Do you know the story of the starfish?" Joy asked me.

Imagine there is a beach full of stranded starfish.

A man is walking along the beach, returning the starfish to the sea…one at a time.

Someone turns to the man and says 'You're not going to make any difference.'

The man picks up another starfish and says 'I made a difference to that one.'

That symbolises Joy's mentality to spending. "While everyone else might be wasting things — if I don't save them, and get every last drop out of everything, then that's one less starfish in the world."

What is Frugality?

Being frugal, does not mean cheap.

Quality and value count.

It is often better to buy something good quality, but more expensive, that lasts a lifetime…than to buy cheaper products that you need to replace every year.

For example, we've always enjoyed the reliability, power and ease of use of the Mac Book Pro Laptops. Moreover, even though they might be three times the price of other laptops, we always buy those so we can work quicker and have less downtime.

We also purchased a solid oak dining table that will outlive us — rather than buying something we'd have to replace every couple of years.

We see Frugal Living as being thrifty with our money, aiming not to pay over the odds for things, particularly if those items or services will not bring joy. We also avoid waste.

However, like the other Millionaires, **we prioritise spending money on things that are important to us**. This is different for everyone.

For instance. We used to feel an element of prestige when we bought all our groceries via Ocado or Waitrose. Let me ask you this — **does the same bottle of champagne taste any better from Waitrose or Tesco?**…of course not.

When we started managing our money better, I put our usual basket of monthly goods into the Tesco app and saved over £300. That's just our basket — you should compare yours. We now shop at Tesco and then **use that £300 saving to pay for a night in a hotel, with Spa, massage and all meals.** It's all about prioritising.

As another example, **perhaps you drink two large lattes a day from a coffee shop** at work (something I used to do). If you kicked that habit and bought your own coffee machine…by the end of the year you'd be able to **use the savings to take a one-week transatlantic cruise from Portsmouth to New York on the QE2.**

One of my friends is a very successful businessman, with a much higher income than ours. He has built and sold companies multiple times.

When we were buying new luxury cars, he was buying higher specification luxury cars that were 1-3 years old —skipping a large part of the depreciation curve. He then put his private car registration plate on them, so you couldn't tell how old they were.

When we bought brand new Lego box sets for our children, he'd buy twice as much off eBay at a fraction of the price.

When he wanted a water butt to collect rainwater, he found a used one advertised locally for free.

I was going to a trendy hair salon once a month. My friend was going to a barber at one-third of the price.

It took me a long time to realise that spending less on unimportant things, enables you to spend lavishly on the things bring you joy.

For nearly all of the Millionaires, **the one item they prioritised the most was personal development**. They were prepared to pay tens of thousands of pounds per year on this.

Andrew said he didn't waste his money on frivolous spending such as cars, watches, and so on — he described himself as "not a lumpy spender."

But Andrew said he was dangerous if he had his credit card at training events, as personal development was once of his greatest interests. Most of the others would agree with that statement. Andrew didn't blindly buy courses — he would run through a cost-benefit analysis in his head before parting with money — how long would it take to pay back?

The Stealth Millionaires paid for mentors, training programs, and books. They regularly attended webinars and listened to audiobooks and podcasts. **They each spent thousands per year on education** and never planned to stop.

The common education themes could be categorised as:
- Property related (as that is what most of them invested in)
- Other income streams (unrelated to property)
- Business
- Mindset
- Health and fitness

The majority of the **Millionaires prioritised living in an upmarket house** that was slightly larger than they needed. It was generally their fourth or fifth home — and at the time, they'd put all of their money into buying it.

Sarah and I also enjoy nice cars, eating out in restaurants and taking day trips during the "working week". We try to lead a stress-free life where we can.

For Linda and Brian, they spend more of their money on new cars, holidays and home furnishings.

Richard prioritises spending his money on holidays and seeing shows at the London theatres. His other big expense is full-time nursery school for his baby boy, costing £1,000 per month — he's looking forward to when he's old enough to get free state schooling. Conversely, his baby boy's favourite things are cake and pudding — so not much expense there!

Every one of the Millionaires I interviewed are frugal. This represents good money management. **None of us dress lavishly or wear designer clothes — we wear whatever we want.**

We don't need to make a statement to impress people. We've already made it. Although we all have a suit and tie in the wardrobe — gathering dust for those occasional outings each year.

I didn't always dress this way. My daily wear was Armani, Versace, Ralph Lauren, Christian Dior, Louis Vuitton and so on. At work I wore tailored suits and shirts.

It took a long time to for me to get over my feelings of inferior status. If I'd have known about the brainwashing to consume products and support the economy, I might have decoupled from designer clothes sooner.

In a line-up, you would be so unlikely to pick out the Millionaires. Only a few of us wear expensive jewellery. In fact, you'd assume we earn less than the "professionals" who have to wear suits for a living. Keep that in mind if you visit a business or property networking meeting.

If I can leave you with some final thoughts on frugality:

- It's better to buy a classically styled quality product that lasts many years (and only buy one), versus buying the latest fashion and having to replace it every season.
- If you only plan to use something once or twice a year, then borrow or rent it.
- If you have to buy it, then does it make any difference at all if you buy it second-hand, at half the price? This enables you to get twice as much value out of every pound you spend.

Buying used is particularly relevant for kid's toys. After a week of playing with any toy, you might as well have bought it second hand in the first place. My son is equally as happy with a games console, whether it's new or second hand.

The majority of the **Stealth Millionaires purchased secondhand items**, for things they deemed less important.

Are You Using a Sieve?

Picture in your mind a tap with water flowing out of it. That is your income.

The **majority of people catch the water with a sieve** — I used to be one of them.

Money is pouring through the holes every day, and they don't even realise it's happening. A lot of spending just grows habitually, or from feeling that it's too much effort to change to cheaper suppliers.

Visiting the coffee shop twice a day, paying to watch the latest movies online, only shopping for groceries at a premium supermarket, buying the latest designer handbag, spending all your spare money on clothes and toys for your baby or children, adding a new subscription for this and that…it all adds up.

As the income from your job increases, you increase your life costs to match it: private schools, luxury holidays, bigger houses, luxury cars. After earning a six-figure salary, you still have **nothing left at the end of the month.**

Conversely, **Stealth Millionaires** don't have a sieve — they **have a Barrel to catch the water**. They aim to get the most value out of every pound they spend.

This can be anything from paying smaller management and trading fees on stocks and shares, to optimising the amount of income and inheritance tax they pay.

It may surprise you to discover that **business owners legitimately pay less personal tax** than employees.

Becoming better educated on company tax regulations and incentives should be one of the key tools for you to get more out of your income. Not only that, but businesses have **unlimited earnings potential** — there's no salary ceiling like there is with a job.

Profit Box

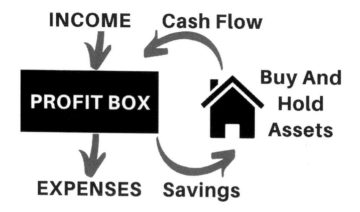

Another concept that can help you to live within your means is to think about your income going into a *Profit Box* — and personal expenses coming out. What's remaining in the box is your profit.

Use surplus profits to invest in assets. Those assets provide cash flow, which generate additional income going into your Profit Box.

It's a virtuous circle, with owning an ever-increasing amount of cash flowing assets, generating larger amounts of income at the top.

Your Profit Box must, must, must, always make profit.

I was talking to someone the other day who told me she never had money left over at the end of the month...and in the same sentence she told me she'd just bought a sofa on finance. NOOOOOOO!

Evaluate your personal expenses as a business. Assuming your Profit Box shows no profits, then you would definitely not approve a few hundred pounds a month for office furniture.

You wouldn't approve a thousand pounds for the latest audio-visual equipment (home TV).

You wouldn't agree to paying for an employee's company car. I met someone whose wife was too sick to work, and he had just been made unemployed.

What was his reaction to this event?

He went out and signed a lease on a new Mercedes convertible! That's nuts!

Another thing I've observed is people borrowing money to pay for their car repairs or service, as they "can't afford it." Then I find out they are off to Spain on holiday for two weeks. Strike off that "employee travel," as you don't have the profit to support it yet.

So, take a look at every pound you spend and imagine your personal life is a business. Remember your Profit Box.

You Can Build Great Wealth on a Small Salary

My father worked as a Senior Charge Nurse in a hospital's surgical theatre and only earned **£22,000 per year**, at the peak of his earnings. That's less than the UK average salary.

He was extremely tight with his money when I was growing up. In fact, I've yet to meet anyone more thrifty than him.

He rarely spent money. He bought his house off the council at a great price and put all of his money into paying it off early. It didn't take him 25 years.

After that, he invested all of his spare money. The returns compounded over the years, as he reinvested the earnings.

He retired at 60 years old due to health reasons. But he had **amassed enough investments and pensions for a very comfortable retirement.**

However, what I didn't realise at the time, was that **he could have retired at least 10 years earlier.** I only discovered this when his health deteriorated further, and he asked me to help manage his finances.

My father did not earn a high salary. He earned less than the average person.

My father lived within his means and re-invested every month.

He could have enjoyed a very comfortable retirement from the age of 50, supporting a family of four.

So, think again if you've been telling yourself that the reason you can't save is because you're not earning enough money.

Every Pound Is a Seedling

> "Every pound is a seedling.
> Invest your seedlings to create a tree.
> Re-invest your seedlings to grow a forest."
>
> —GEORGE CHOY
> PROPERTY INVESTOR & AUTHOR

Every time I spend money, I think about the opportunity cost. **My brain thinks in houses** — I can't help it!! For example, let's say I was about to spend £15,000 on something. Well that amount could be used instead as deposit on a £50,000 house that will pay me at least £250 per month.

If I was going to spend £5,000 then my brain tells me it's a third of the cash required to buy a house.

Whatever you invest in, make it a habit to start to calculate the return you could achieve on that money each time you reach for your wallet.

Linda and Brian were the only Millionaires not looking to grow their investments further, being the oldest of the group, at 70 years old. They are enjoying spending all the income they receive from their property portfolio and pensions.

Bad Debt Versus Good Debt

Firstly, not all debt is bad.

Bad debt could be considered anything with a high interest rate. With interest rates currently at the lowest in history, then anything above 12% could be considered expensive. It depends…

Generally, the worst offenders are pay day loans, credit cards, overdraft, unregulated finance and some personal loans.

Bad debt gets out of control. This is intentional, as the interest rates are so high that you can be hooked to them forever. You may find that every year you owe more than before.

Andrew had over £90,000 in credit card debt many years ago. Initially he was transferring it from one 0% interest card to another…but there came a point when he couldn't transfer it anymore and it became bad debt. He took steps to clear it. When his income went up, or mortgage repayments went down — he made a point of using this extra money to pay off the bad debt first.

I've been there too. When I was 23 I had about £400 outstanding on a credit card and I was only paying the minimum amount each month. I never had any money left at the end of the month, so the balance barely reduced. I was earning about £1,300 a month at the time — the problem was that I spent all my wages on going out with friends and buying designer clothes.

Many years later I worked for a credit card company and my eyes started to open. Maybe you're not aware, but if you only pay off the minimum payment each month then you'll probably be paying that for the next 20 years or more.

And if you get out another credit card and do the same, then that's another 20 years for that too.

So, if you're facing the dilemma of whether to save 10% each month, or pay 10% off your bad debts, then **I always recommend clearing the bad debt first**. I would rather spend nothing and become a hermit for months on end to clear it as fast as possible, than have it limp on for 20 years.

If it's on a credit card, then you may be able to transfer the balance to a 0% interest card for a year. However, unless you continue to pay it off, then you are only delaying the problem.

What you should do in future, is always pay off your credit cards 100% in full every month. Set them to automatically debit from your bank. If you can't afford to buy something, then don't spend the money in the first place!

However, I would like to take this further. **I consider bad debt as any loan used to spend on consumables or depreciating assets.**

For example, this could be a loan to pay for a car, holiday or new kitchen. I once knew someone with a low income who got a £20,000 loan to pay for their wedding and honeymoon. That is crazy person thinking! Spending £20,000 for one day…on people that you barely know… to end up in debt for years.

On the other side of the coin is Good Debt.

Good debt is used to invest in assets, such as buying an investment property. Or it could be as a loan to expand your profitable business. You must have a great deal of certainty that the income you receive will be able to pay off the loan each month, before committing to the loan.

Don't take on debt for peer-to-peer lending, gambling, or to invest in the stock market or cryptocurrencies. None of these provide a 100 per cent guaranteed return that will service the monthly loan payments.

Do you have any credit at all? I've met a number of people that are proud that they don't have any debt or facilities for debt. What they don't realise is that this lowers their credit score, as the lenders feel you are not experienced in managing your money. You might get declined for something so simple as a mobile phone contract.

Therefore, you should take out credit in your own name — not as the second person on your partner's account. Get your own credit card and make sure you pay it off in full every month. Also make sure at least one of the utility bills is in your name, as this helps with validating your identity during credit checks.

It's essential to **check your credit report** as a substantial proportion of people have errors on their file, such as outstanding debts that they paid off many years ago. There are plenty of free providers on the internet where you can check your credit score:

- moneysavingexpert.com/creditclub
- clearscore.com
- creditkarma.co.uk

Get Your Partner on Board

If they are complete **shopaholics** (like I was), then **it will take time to get them living within their means** and investing instead.

Try not to judge them. They have not financially evolved into the Millionaire mindset yet. That's ok. I was just like them.

You may need to hold separate bank accounts in the beginning, so that one partner doesn't spend the other partner's savings.

My father had to keep control of the majority of the money to avoid my mother spending it all — that turned out to be a good strategy for them, as he became very successful at investing and securing them a comfortable retirement.

You both have an amazing opportunity right now. I didn't learn these lessons for many years. You can apply them right now and be financially secure for the rest of your life. You'll be able to survive recessions, stock market crashes and whatever pandemics or disasters happen in the world.

The first step is to **tell them the benefits**. If you're thinking about starting a family, then imagine what it will be like when you don't need to work…you could spend all day watching your baby grow up and say their first word or take their first steps. You wouldn't miss a thing.

If you already have children, you may be feeling guilty about being at work all day. So, you spend all your money on them to make sure they have the best start in life…

But think about what life would be like if you could spend every waking moment with them instead?

Building your relationship is worth much more to them than any amount of money you can spend, to relieve your guilt.

Encourage your partner to read this book. Then **lead by example** and show them how much you are saving and investing.

If you're single, then maybe you just want to travel the world. That's ok too.

The important thing is to **visualise what your life will be like when you can do whatever you want.**

Or if you still want to work, because you do a job that helps people and gives your life purpose, then at least you can be financially secure in case you are too unwell to work or lose your job.

Chapter Two Summary:
Live below Your Means

- Be frugal with your spending. Buy second hand, rent or borrow. Get more out of every pound
- Don't upgrade your lifestyle
- Catch your income streams in a Barrel, not a Sieve
- Profit Box — your personal finances are a business
- You can build great wealth on a small salary
- Every pound is a potential seedling to invest
- Eliminate your bad debt
- Use good debt to buy income producing assets
- Check your credit report
- Get your partner on board with saving and investing

CHAPTER THREE:

Low-Key Life

Prioritise Your Financial Independence over Displaying Wealth

> "To Become Rich – You Must Value Saving More than Spending."
>
> —GEORGE CHOY
> PROPERTY INVESTOR & AUTHOR

Don't Have — Be and Do Instead

Trinkets are useless to you when you die, so stop wasting time buying lots of stuff.

Bronnie Ware looked after patients in the final months, or weeks of their lives. She asked the patients what they most regretted in their lives and published the common themes in her book—*The top five regrets of the dying:*

1. I wish I'd had the courage to live a life true to myself, not the life others expected of me
2. I wish I hadn't worked so much

3. I wish I'd had the courage to express my feelings
4. I wish I had stayed in touch with my friends
5. I wish that I had let myself be happier

Have you noticed how none of the regrets are about something they wish they'd bought?

There's no Rolex, Ferrari, private jet or mansion on the list. What is on the list is what they wanted to be, what they wanted to do, and maintaining relationships. Keep the end in mind and focus on that instead of trinkets.

Experiences ranked very highly with the Stealth Millionaires. Most of them focused on holidays, and to a lesser extent, entertainment, such as days out and going to the theatre.

Sacrifice — Be Willing to Do What Others Won't Do

It takes a lot of sacrifice to become a Millionaire. If it was easy, then everyone would be a Millionaire.

The most obvious sacrifice is living way below your means and using all remaining funds to invest in income producing assets and investments. You may have to give up expensive holidays for a while.

Other people won't be doing this. They will be actively encouraging you to spend more money like them. It will be tough to resist.

Don't think you can maintain your current spending habits, to become a Millionaire. It just won't happen.

There must be sacrifice. And the more you sacrifice, the faster it happens.

You won't just need to sacrifice how you spend your money, **you'll also need to forfeit your time**. You will need to learn about your chosen investment strategies, and spend time implementing them.

I remember working ten hours a day in London, plus two hours of commuting. Sarah and I spent most of our weekends either looking for property or renovating them.

There were a couple of times when we were tiling a bathroom or painting walls throughout the night, so we could get the job finished over the weekend.

We now outsource all the refurbishments, as it is faster and you get a better job than trying to DIY. But there is still work to do.

For example, when we add a new property to our portfolio we spend time…finding and viewing properties, agreeing the purchase, liaising with our solicitor, raising finance, refurbishing and finally working with a letting agent to get a tenant moved in.

However, once that's done, we can sit back and put our feet up…and let the cash roll in, forever.

You will also need to **sacrifice the time you spend with your current friends**. You get a whole different quality of conversation when you are hanging around with millionaires, rather than those with a poor mindset. Spending more time with people that have trodden the path already, is a faster way to reach it than going it alone.

You tend to talk more about investing, saving tax and improving yourself and your business through education.

The Rise of Consumption Culture

The roots of consumption began with the invention of mass production.

In 1913, Henry Ford, the founder of the Ford Motor Company, launched a major innovation to manufacture the Ford Model T — the moving assembly line.

Mass production techniques were then adopted across most industries during the 1920s.

In 1922, Henry Ford said "We want the man who buys one of our cars never to have to buy another. We never make an improvement that renders any previous model obsolete."

The US President Calvin Coolidge was seen as the embodiment of frugality and had inspired others to do the same. In his autobiography, he wrote: "There is no dignity quite so impressive, and no one independence quite so important, as living within your means."

Goods were built to last. The masses had been encouraged to take care of their possessions.

That was **creating an unforeseen problem**.

The 1920s were not a good time for most, as 60% of people lived below the poverty line.
In the January 1927 edition of Nation's Business magazine, an article by James L. Wright led with:

> **"Need We Be Afraid of a Job Famine?**
> The Department of Labor gives out some surprising figures showing how the machine is replacing the man. Is there a danger of working ourselves out of work?"

In an interview with Secretary James J. Davis from the United States Department of Labor, Davis stated:

> "We already have the problem of overproduction or under-consumption."

> "The textile mills of this country can produce all the cloth needed in six months' operation each year."

> "14 per cent of the boot and shoe factories in the United States…could produce all the footwear needed."

> "3 per cent of the present flour mills could produce all the flour needed."

So, the United States was at cross-roads. **Either they allowed mass unemployment** to continue to grow, **or they needed to increase people's consumption** of goods. They were potentially on the brink of economic disaster.

Enter their saviour, **Edward Bernays — nephew of Sigmund Freud,** the father of psychoanalysis.

During World War I, Bernays worked for the Committee of Public Information. His remit was to build support for the war, both in the US and abroad. Drawing on Freud's work, Bernays referred to his **use of publicity techniques to manipulate the masses as "psychological warfare."**

In 1928 Bernays published the book *"Propaganda."* There were a lot of negative connotations with that word, so he coined a new term to describe it for use in peacetime, *Public Relations.*

Freud's research into the unconscious mind brought him to the conclusion that human beings were too dangerous to think for themselves.

Bernays agreed. In order for a democratic society to successfully exist, **the masses needed to be manipulated by elite leadership, to control what the masses think and do.**

> "The conscious and intelligent **manipulation of organized habits and opinions of the masses** is an important element in democratic society.

Those who manipulate this unseen mechanism
of society constitute an invisible government
which is the true ruling power of our country."

"It is **they who pull the wires which control
the public mind.**"

President Hoover had consulted with Bernays a number
of times to sell policy ideas and campaigns.

At a speech to Advertising executives, President Hoover
stated, "You have taken over the job of **creating desire**
and have transformed people into **constantly moving
happiness machines**, machines which have become the
key to economic progress."

Bernays noted that by stimulating desires and satisfying
them with the happiness of consumption, in an endless
loop, it also had the beneficial effect **making the
masses docile.**

Manufacturers decided to increase consumer
consumption through two key strategies:
1) Making sure products didn't last as long,
   becoming more disposable.
2) "Beauty" — creating new designs every year or
   more, in order to perceive goods as being out of
   date.

One notable example of Bernays work, was
encouraging women to smoke, at a time when it was
only socially acceptable for men to smoke.

He consulted for the American Tobacco Industry to solve the market opportunity. He engineered slender and beautiful debutantes to light up during a parade and communicated to the press that they were lighting their "Torches of freedom". This powerful signal made it a sign of women's independence and freedom of rights.

Bernays was famous for **employing psychologists and doctors to do studies, which were not impartial**.

He was behind the notion of the "all American" breakfast being associated with bacon and eggs. His campaigns convinced doctors to tell their patients it was "healthy" to eat bacon and eggs for breakfast.

Even **the desire to wear fashionable clothes has been engineered**. People used to just wear clothes. They were just functional. You had a hat. A coat. A shirt. A handbag.

The PR machine spurred up to make it unacceptable to do that, otherwise you would be mundane, and look the same as everyone else.

He helped **create the illusion** that you were **inferior if you didn't express your individuality through fashion**…which led to people regularly buying more clothes and accessories. That solved the textile manufacturing surplus.

In later years, Bernays worked with President Eisenhower to increase consumer spending. Bernays convinced him to **promote the fear of communism**, and **make it everyone's national duty to spend, spend, spend.**

There were billboards during the Great Depression depicting people driving cars. They stated:

> "World's highest standard of living.
> There's no way like the American Way"

In case you think using the ad men to increase consumer consumption due to over-production, couldn't possibly occur today, then think again. The FDA and the USDA fund various trade associations.

One of which is a National Dairy Checkoff program, which has funded advertising to shift stockpiles of cheese, created from the over-production of milk. This led to the creation of Pizza Hut's stuffed-crust pizza.

I'd like to leave you with this final thought on spending…

It's not your fault that you have a continual desire to spend and consume.

You are the **victim of "Public Relations"**, designed to subdue the masses and fuel the economy, jobs and taxes.

You've been brainwashed. So, take off your blindfold and **stop spending money on sh*t you can't afford!**

Conspicuous Consumption

This term describes the purchasing of luxury goods and services to enhance your social status.

I am also partly to blame for fuelling desire in others. In the past, I was responsible for marketing the top global luxury brands to high net worth individuals. I arranged private events to get them to part with their money. Lots of celebrities, fine wines, champagne and catwalk models.

I remember sitting at a private dinner I'd arranged at a well-known luxury jeweller in London. The store was closed, and throughout the dinner the guests would go off and pay £25,000 for a watch that was coming soon.

There were other events, where they'd drive a super car around a test track, and then put down a deposit whilst they were there. Spending over £100,000 in an afternoon, seemed like the thing to do.

I was also conned. I'll be the first to put my hands up. **I was stuck the Conspicuous Consumption trap** for decades.

I started off just spending all my money on the latest gadgets, clothes and so on. Later, when I studied for a Masters in Business Administration (MBA) at university, my peers were all wealthy international students.

The international student's lifestyles were fully funded by their parents (who were much richer than mine), so it was normal for them to only wear designer clothes and accessories.

And so began my addiction to buying luxury fashion brands such as Armani, Versace, and so on…as a student!

Things got worse when I worked at a financial services company in the City. **You were expected to spend a lot of money.**

Everyone would brag about how they just bought the latest, most expensive designer handbag, or went to a new Michelin star restaurant, or went on the most luxurious holiday ever. I upgraded to tailor made suits and shirts, as well as designer accessories.

I'm not alone. Richard had similar experiences when he was a management consultant. He was encouraged to spend more by his colleagues.

He estimated he blew £1,000 a month on meaningless stuff. Once he got called into his manager's office and was asked to buy another tailor-made shirt — as the one he was wearing wasn't looking pristine anymore.

One of the best things for my wallet was to quit my job and start a business working from home. No more suits or the need to buy designer clothes. Hello jeans, t-shirts and gym gear. I also felt less pressure to spend.

I wondered if maybe I was the only person who preferred to wear joggers at home? But during the

Coronavirus outbreak, many clothes retailers reported increased sales of sweatpants and hooded tops. So I'm not alone!

All of our **Stealth Millionaires dress in whatever they want** and don't care what people think. They dress for comfort. Most wear trainers every day and don't try to look flash. They wear mass market brands. Clothing with badges on are less important to them.

Consider Facebook's co-founder Mark Zuckerberg, worth over $54 billion. He has a closet full of identical grey t-shirts and blue jeans.

CEO of VaynerMedia, Gary Vaynerchuk, is worth over $160 million, is always seen in a t-shirt or hoodie, jeans and trainers.

If you didn't know who those two people were, you would quite easily pass them on the street, completely unaware of their vast wealth.

Happiness Set Point and the Hedonic Treadmill

In psychology, the theory of the *Happiness Set Point* is that **we all have a baseline of happiness** that we return to throughout life.

Some people may experience life with the 'glass half-full' and others with the 'glass half-empty' — they have a higher or lower natural happiness set point.

For example, if you are always miserable and you win the lottery…then your positivity will be short-lived, and you will return to your normal state of misery again.

The ***Hedonic Treadmill*** or *Hedonic Adaptation* refers to the **process of getting used to positive or negative events.** For example, you know how you feel excited to buy a new mobile phone…it's so shiny, it has a better camera, it does much more, and you just can't wait! You feel excited for a little time, then shortly return back to your happiness set point.

On the other hand, there are times when things go wrong. Perhaps you get the flu. You feel negative for many days, with a runny nose, fever and just feeling downright awful. But eventually you get better and return to your happiness set point.

HEDONIC TREADMILL

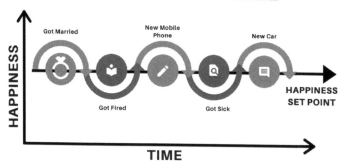

Both the **amount of happiness and duration of the emotion, varies according to the event**. So, getting married will last longer than buying a new outfit.

Once you're aware that peaks can vary, then **there are ways you can stretch the duration of the peaks**, to make the happiness last a bit longer.

For example, do you remember buying your first car — you were probably very happy for months. Every time you drove it you felt great. The car brought with it a lot of independence that you didn't have before, when you relied on public transportation and getting rides from your friends.

When you buy your next car, the feeling of joy only lasts for a month or two before returning to your set point. And if your car is basically the same as the last one, then the peak can be even smaller.

Putting all this together, means that if the thing you buy will completely change your life (like your first car), then don't spend too much on the first one. When you get your second car, you can upgrade a little, but not too much...and so on. If instead you went straight for the Ferrari for your first car, then you would lose the joy of cars pretty quickly.

I really wish I'd known that before. My first car was a brand-new BMW that I really couldn't afford, and it put me into bad debt. It led to a domino of one luxury car after another.

Another way of really lengthening the curve is to find a way to keep improving the item. For example, perhaps you buy a house which needs a lot of work and you spend the next five years fixing it up slowly, one room at a time. Your enjoyment will extend.

A word of caution, **there can also be positive peaks that end with a longer negative effect** —

For example, let's say you took out a **10-year loan to pay for your wedding**. On the long build up to the wedding you are really excited. The day is magical. After a couple of months, the wedding seems like a distant memory and you start to feel the impact of that debt. Unexpected costs happen, or your income drops, and you start to regret signing up for a loan in the first place. The positive **wedding day peak then starts to go negative.**

The same thing can happen with car finance, if you choose a car you really can't afford.

But, there is a pot of gold at the end of the Hedonic Treadmill. **If you fix a substantial source of unhappiness** in your life, then this **happiness peak could last for years!**

For example. We used to live in a house in the countryside that was slightly smaller than we needed, and it was a 15 minute drive from our children's school.

This really irked Sarah. Every time she took the kids to and from school, she got annoyed. She wanted to get back to walking them to school, like we did in our previous home. And if we wanted to go to the shops, we had to drive again.

It was a year of unhappiness for Sarah, before she said enough was enough, and we moved to a new house within walking distance of both the school and shops. After seven months, she still feels grateful every time she walks to town.

So, remember the Hedonic Treadmill the next time you think about parting with cash for something you "really want." **The excitement will be brief and won't bring as much joy as you think** — and if you're taking out a loan or finance, then the negative curve can last many years after the excitement has gone.

You Don't Need a Huge Amount of Money to Live on

When I've mentored people or been invited to speak at conferences, I often ask people for their financial freedom figure. What's yours?

Have a think for a moment…

The crowd nearly always say £5,000 or £10,000 per month. This figure isn't built on reality, it's just how much they "think" they need to live on.

It's funny how everyone comes up with the same numbers. I guess it's like when you ask people to think of a vegetable…
…which vegetable are you thinking of?

Is it a carrot?

No, I'm not a mind reader.

Okay, back to the serious stuff. I bet you're wondering...how much do WE spend?

Well, let's put it into context. Sarah and I currently have one car that we own outright and live in a 4 double-bedroom house in a nice upmarket neighbourhood. We have two children and a cat. We subscribe to Netflix. We eat out regularly in restaurants and take day trips to entertain ourselves when our children are at school.

We typically spend an average of £4,200 per month. That doesn't include the transfers to savings — that's just our expenditure.

Of that spend, £1,600 is for the rent on the house we live in, so the remaining personal spend is only £2,600 per month. Probably a lot lower than you thought?

But how far could YOU take it?...

We occasionally challenge ourselves to have a "no spend" month. If we don't do anything at all...no meals out, barely driving the car, eating the cupboards bare, only doing things that are free — we can get this down to £2,738 in a single month!

This means that after deducting rent, we only spent £1,138. Remember, this is a family of four in a nice house. Consequently, it is possible to do an extreme cut back of the expenses and put an extra £1,500 into savings each month. This is a very useful strategy if you are in bad debt, as it will help you to clear it faster.

It just goes to show how much money people fritter away each month. If you're single or a couple, you could do way better than us.

Stealth Millionaires typically spent £2,500 to £4,500 per month on living expenses.

Let's let those figures sink in.

Some of you are spending more than that per month, and you are not millionaires yet...**perhaps that is why you are not.**

It's also not the £10,000 per month that people think millionaires are spending, to be flashy with their wealth. They are investing the difference — not spending it.

Shop for Assets, Not Sh*t

> "People buy feelings, not things"
>
> —TONY ROBBINS

Hey, I've been there myself. **Buying sh*t to impress people I don't like...or know...so I could feel significant**.

What car do you drive?

What's your favourite brand of clothing?

The main problem with spending all your money on sh*t, is that you don't increase your wealth. And if you go too far, you'll end up having to sell the important stuff, to get you out of a hole.

Once you've spent the money, it's gone.

A much better strategy, which all of our Stealth Millionaires follow, is to invest in assets first. The income from those assets can then pay for the priorities in your lifestyle.

None of the Stealth Millionaires went shopping for the day. They didn't hang out in malls — aimlessly wandering around and spending their cash. They only went out to buy what they had already pre-planned, then went home. We generally shop online.

Invest in Property First, Before Spending

Our favourite asset class is Property. As the saying goes "Don't wait to buy property, buy property and wait."

We shop for houses, not shoes. Let's assume you buy a cheap house for £50,000. Yes, it is still possible to do that in many parts of the UK. You decide to apply for a mortgage, which means you only put down £12,500 cash for the deposit.

Now **imagine that house posting £250 cheques through your letterbox every month.** I can't imagine £12,500 cars doing that!

Big Wins — Cars and Houses

These two are usually the biggest expenses for most people, so they can also provide the biggest win to your finances.

Let's start with cars.

Second Car
Firstly, do you have more than one car? If so, how often do you actually drive it?

We used to have a second car. But **I probably only used it once or twice a month** to go to the train station. I was paying out for depreciation, car tax, servicing, insurance, tyres, etc.

We worked out that we could save thousands per year by selling our second car — plus we would get some cash in the bank.

Consequently, Sarah **advertised for a local driver** on social media, and I now pay them to take me to the station and collect me when I return. It's much more cost-effective.

But do you really need a car at all?
When Richard lived in London he chose not to own a car. He mostly used public transport. On those occasional days where he needed a car to go to Ikea, **he**

hired a car from the car club he remains a member of. The annual subscription is now £60. Richard (being an early joiner) pays nothing for membership of the car club — he just pays for the hours he hires.

Andrew shares a car with his son. Andrew pays the monthly lease costs, and his son pays for maintenance.

Car Brands
Cars are not assets; they lose money every day that passes — that's why **I don't include them in my net worth calculations.** When you think about it, you are literally renting the ability to get around, even if you "own it."

Conversely, some classic cars are investments as they appreciate in value. But you shouldn't rack up miles in classic cars, otherwise they will lose value — so, you'll still need to buy another car anyway, which kind of defeats the purpose.

All of our Millionaires could sell one or two houses to buy a Ferrari or other supercar — **but none had.**

Most of the Stealth Millionaires did not drive a luxury car. They drove everyday brands such as Hyundai, Toyota and Kia. Although Linda and Brian had a Mercedes and Joy drove an Audi.

Sarah and I were the only ones that have owned a string of luxury cars (my fault). At the time of writing this book we were driving a Hyundai MPV — although

Sarah and I have constant disagreements about whether to get another Land Rover next time.

Age of the car
A new car will typically depreciate by 50-60% within the first three years. I've personally made some stupid mistakes when it comes to cars! Like buying a Land Rover Discovery for £42,000 in cash, and selling it three years later, losing £20,000 in depreciation. I'm sure it would be a frightening number to add up the total money I've lost on car depreciation over the years.

It was one of my favourite cars to drive, but I wasn't smart with my money. It also wasn't the first time I'd bought a brand-new car with cash and sold it within three years, losing a huge chunk of cash.

A consistent theme of the Stealth Millionaires that preferred to own, was to **either buy new and keep for up to ten years** (to ride out the depreciation curve) **or buy cars at least three years old.** That's smart.

Buying versus leasing
You'll need to weigh this up. On the plus side, leasing means that you don't need to put up a large chunk of cash. That appeals to me, as I now see the opportunity cost of using chunks of cash as deposits on houses. Each brand-new car could buy at least one house with a mortgage.

For example, at the time of writing, you could buy a £50,000 house with only £12,500 deposit. That would pay enough rent to cover the cost of a monthly lease on a £38,000 BMW 4 Series Grand Diesel Coupe. In addition, let's not forget that the house will increase in value, and the rent will go up over the years. So, effectively you could drive a car for free.

If you plan to own brand-new cars for three years, then leasing is probably a better option. In the UK, every member of an LLP can have a company car. **You might save money by leasing a company car** and expensing most of the costs — just like Richard does. Speak to your accountant or tax expert.

Whatever you decide to do, consider the opportunity cost of investing the money instead.

Personal Houses – Renting versus Buying

> "Rent where you live, and own what you can rent to others."
>
> —GRANT CARDONE

In the UK, we've grown up being told that we should all own our homes. Society tells us we are considered poor if we are not homeowners. One of the variables in your credit score is whether or not you own. However, in other markets like Germany, most people are renters.

Interestingly, one of the questions Sarah and I get asked a lot, is **"why are we living in a rented house?"**

Sarah and I owned what we considered our "forever home" situated in a stockbroker town, just over half an hour train ride to London. It was a converted tractor barn, over 170 years old with oak beams and flooring.

We had refurbished it and put in a loft conversion, to increase its value. We never thought we would ever sell this house in our lifetime.

As we were thinking more and more about the opportunity cost of holding chunks of cash, instead of investing, one day it hit us...

We could sell our home and invest the proceeds to buy four rental properties. Those four properties would provide enough income to rent a home of the same standard, AND fund at least half of our living costs. So we could live in the same house, and get paid to live there!

For some people, **that could be the equivalent of your annual salary**...so you wouldn't need to work anymore.

Richard, the wealthiest of our Stealth Millionaires, with £15 million of investment properties, **is also a renter**. His rationale is the same as ours. Why tie up so much cash? Invest instead.

One of the other advantages of renting rather than owning is flexibility. Need to move area? Need a larger or smaller house? No problem, you can move with minimal cost and fuss. No need to wait to sell, just pick your new house and off you go.

Grand Cardone is worth over $300 million. Does he own his home? No. **He rents too.**

> "The secret to success is to own nothing, but control everything"
>
> —NELSON ROCKEFELLER

One of the other **benefits of not owning your home**, is having **no assets in your personal name**.

Have all your investment assets owned by a company or trust instead. And by having multiple companies, each with a different stream of income, you can ringfence and protect them from potential harm.

Keeping housing costs down
Your home is generally not an income producing asset. It sucks money out of you every month in mortgage payments, utility bills, insurance, maintenance, tax, etc. It doesn't pay money into your bank account each month, like investments can.
As people get promotions or bonuses, they tend to upgrade their lifestyle, which includes bigger and nicer houses.

One of the issues with getting bigger and **nicer houses**, is to keep up with the **cost of the lifestyle that comes with it**.

I remember when Sarah and I bought a four-bedroom house before we had children. We had to make up a use for all the spare rooms and fill them with furniture and other doodads. **We barely used these rooms**.

Maintenance and household bills also cost more on the bigger houses — it's **the hidden cost of ownership**.

People imagine millionaires living in on a country estate. However, the Stealth Millionaires tended to live in a nice four-bedroom house, not a six-bedroom mansion.

This was slightly larger than they needed, as they usually had one or two bedrooms empty. **They weren't planning to upgrade to bigger houses.** Most were intending to stay in the same house for at least ten or more years, and were considering downsizing when they got older.

If you want to get to Millionaire status quicker, it can be a good idea to keep your home costs lower and then invest in assets instead of upgrading. **You can get your bigger house later if you want.**

On the other hand, I do have a fantasy on my Dream Board of buying a grand house and having multiple generations living there at the same time. That would have been useful during the Coronavirus pandemic, as we would all have been able to see each other.

Alternatively, buying a farm and building our own village with four houses for ourselves, our children and grandparents, with shared facilities, such as a gym, swimming pool, and so on. Time will tell.

Lower cost places to live
You might also contemplate **moving to a lower-cost area**, particularly if you don't need to live in a particular area to make a living.

That's also one of the changes we made, when we decided to sell our house and move into rented accommodation. We moved to an equally nice town, but further away from London where the cost of renting was lower.

There's also an argument for moving closer to your place of work, if the difference cuts down the travel cost enough to compensate for the cost of housing.

Also consider living in a smaller property and don't trade up. You could live in a house share.

Conversely, you could buy a bigger house than you need, and **rent the remaining rooms to lodgers**. One of our friends Nicky does this, and it pays for the cost of her mortgage and all of her utility bills. Effectively, she gets the house for free.

Doodads, Stuff and Minimalism

> "I recommend you dispose of anything that does not fall into one of three categories: currently in use, needed for a limited period of time, or must be kept indefinitely"
>
> — MARIE KONDO
> THE LIFE-CHANGING MAGIC OF TIDYING UP

I think that is great advice. **We all have a natural tendency to buy stuff and hoard it**…just in case.

If you need a computer cable with an unusual connector, I probably have one in the large box that sits in my office cupboard. I reduced the number of cables by half a year ago, but there's still a lot in there! We also have a whole drawer of various free and purchased pens. I'm sure there are things you hoard as well.

Overall **our house and car are always very tidy**, and there isn't much in our attic. Given that we have two kids under 10 years old, that's no easy feat!

Having lots of **clutter makes it difficult to concentrate** — it can be distracting and reduce your happiness. Your subconscious brain will be constantly thinking "I really should tidy that," whenever you are trying to focus on something. It will pop into your head hundreds of times per day. It's weighing you down.

Think carefully before buying anything to add to the mess. **Should you buy, borrow or rent it?** Or **buy it second-hand** and then resell it as soon as you've finished with it?

Understand the difference between "wants" or desires, and "needs." You might want a luxury car, but you only need a car, or perhaps don't actually need it at all.

You could write your wants on a list and see whether you still want them in a month.

Remember the Hedonic Treadmill. Your happiness from buying the doodads won't last long.

This doesn't mean you can't buy them. Just do as the rich do — **buy assets to pay for the doodads.**

Want a Ferrari?

Invest first and use the monthly income to pay for the leasing costs. As an example, three of my rental houses in the South of England would cover the cost of leasing a Ferrari.

Want to take a couple of holidays each year? Do the same thing — buy a rental property or invest in the stock market to pay for it out of your cashflow.

Every time you want to **upgrade your lifestyle, invest in assets first, before spending.**

Chapter Three Summary:
Low-Key Life

- Prioritise your Financial Independence over displaying your wealth
- Trinkets are useless to you when you die. Live your dream life — spend it doing what's important, and with the important people in your life
- You will need to sacrifice to become a Millionaire — but you can relax once you've made it
- Hedonic Treadmill - happiness is short-lived. Debt can outlast the happiness of buying something
- You've been brainwashed to spend and consume, in order to create a happiness loop, that makes the masses docile and props up the economy, jobs and taxes
- Spend less on your home. Or rent instead
- Be sensible with cars
- Stop spending money on sh*t you can't afford
- You don't need a huge amount of Money to live on
- Shop for assets, not sh*t.
- Invest first, before spending

CHAPTER FOUR:

Invest

Become Recession-proof with Multiple Streams of Income

One thing is certain. **Black swan events can damage your income.** These are completely unpredictable…but anticipated. We've had Swine Flu, Ebola and the Coronavirus. There are hurricanes, tornados, earthquakes, tsunamis and flooding.

Industries fall into decline. Government or tax regulations change.

There will be a recession.

The stock market will crash.

The housing market will freefall…

…but they also recover. And over the long-term, both the stock market and average house prices, continue to grow.

The average age when people buy their first home continues to rise, as the gap between house prices and wages widens.

Your job is not for life. **You have no job security.**

You could be made redundant **or lose all of your income** at any time.

The first way to combat that is to **have a passive income stream that doesn't rely on trading your time for money.**

The second way to protect against disasters is to **have multiple streams of income.**

Think about it this way. Assume **each leg of a chair is an income stream**. If you're sitting on it and one leg gets snapped off, you should still be able to sit on it without falling over.

However, **if you only had one or two legs, then you're going to crash on the floor.**

Most people only have one income stream — their job.

However, most Millionaires have multiple income streams. In general, **our Stealth Millionaires had 3-5 income streams** and they were all interested in having more. Our findings were similar to Tom Corley's Rich Habits study of 100 millionaires, which found that 65 per cent had 3 streams of income.

Whilst it's better from a retirement perspective to have all of your income streams completely passive, there is room for a trading business.

A trading business will take up your time, but it could be anything. In an ideal world it would be something you love doing and wouldn't count as "work".

For example, perhaps you can consult on a project, do public speaking for money, run training sessions, flip things on eBay, sell widgets on Amazon, decorate someone's house, source property deals, manage someone else's rental property, or refurbish and flip properties.

This shouldn't be a get rich quick business. It really doesn't matter what you choose, as long as it is profitable. You can then **feed the profits from your trading business straight into your investments** — remember, invest before spending.

The other advantage of having a trading business in addition to passive income, is you can do as much, or as little of it as you want. And if you have a really bad month from all of your other income streams, you can choose to do more work in your trading business to top up your Profit Box.

But…if you can **create a fully systemised trading business**, that requires almost no input from you, then that will be a great source of passive income. For example, some sort of monthly subscription model.

Asset Classes — Like and Understand

As you'll recall from the Introduction chapter, the **top two sources of wealth from The Sunday Times Rich List were property and investments.** These are proven strategies to become Financially Free. So, we'll start with those two, and then I'll give you one more, Intellectual Property.

Whatever you decide to invest in, be aware that like all investments, the income and value of your fund can go up, as well as down. There is always risk. But one could argue that the risk of doing nothing is even greater.

1) PROPERTY

Property (or Real Estate) has many different strategies. I consider each of them a different stream of income, as black swan events do not usually hit all of them to the same extent. And government regulations or tax changes usually only target one strategy, not the whole industry.

Sarah and I currently do four of the strategies below. So, if one leg of the stool breaks, we still have three left to sit on.

- Residential rentals: Buy to Let
- House in Multiple Occupation (HMO)
- Serviced Accommodation (or Furnished Holiday Let)
- Property Development and Commercial to Residential Conversions
- Commercial Property Investing

There are other property strategies, but the end users are mostly variations of the above.

I don't include my private residence in this list. Owning a home is not a cash flow generating asset. It sucks money out of you every month.

My personal preference is property above all other assets.

My reason is that unlike the stock market, where the value of your fund is going up and down every second of the day, property takes longer for valuation changes. You don't need to sell off properties to get income (unless you are flipping or developing), as **the rentals pay you income every month.**

For step-by-step instructions on how to invest in property, see our other book:
RETIRE NOW! Your Blueprint to Financial Freedom Through Property.
mycastleproperty.co.uk/books

2) INVESTMENTS – STOCKS & SHARES

> "If you aren't willing to own a stock for ten years, don't even think about owning it for ten minutes."
>
> — WARREN BUFFETT
> BILLIONAIRE INVESTOR

One of the benefits of investing in the stock market, versus property, is that **you don't need much money to start.** You could just pay in £100 per month.

And if you decide to invest in property later, then you could cash in some of your stocks and shares to do it.

My father was a big advocate of the stock market and it gave him a comfortable, early retirement.

Like all strategies, there are **get rich quick schemes**, like day trading or investing in the next cryptocurrency. **I recommend you avoid them**.

It is gambling. I prefer to know my income is certain and it can pump out money while I sleep. I don't want the stress of checking my investments every second of the day.

If you don't believe me, then take the advice of **billionaire Ray Dalio**, who **manages the largest hedge**

fund in the world. In an interview with Tony Robbins discussing day trading in the stock market, Ray said:[4]

> "But you can't do it by trying to beat the system. You don't want to try. I have fifteen hundred employees and forty years of experience, and it's a tough game for me.
>
> **This is poker with the best poker players on earth**."

But what about asking a broker or a mutual fund manager to invest your money? Ray thinks this is a bad idea.

> "typical money managers are not going to help you win because they don't have the skills or resources to play in the big game, either."
>
> "If they did, you wouldn't have access to them."

And if you still have any doubts about investing for the long-term, look at Warren Buffet. He is currently the fourth wealthiest person on the planet, and **he only invests for the long-term.**

So, given that you should not try to time the market, what kind of stocks and shares should you buy?

The answer is stupidly simple. It's what Warren Buffet recommends to investors, and **the same path that**

---

[4] Money Master the Game

many other people have followed to become financially free.

You simply **invest in a low-cost index tracker**, using a company that also has **low management fees**. You must check the charges for both.

Although most fund managers quote high returns, they also take hefty fees which negate many of those returns. Trackers are near enough automated, so that's why the running costs are very low indeed.

Trackers also diversify your investment across multiple companies.

For example, you might decide to get an S&P 500 tracker (as recommended by Warren Buffet), or a FTSE 250 tracker in the UK.

An accumulation tracker can be useful in the early years, to build the fund, before switching to an income tracker later.

Aim to **pay in the same amount every month, to even out the market fluctuations**. Don't try to time the market or put in a huge lump sum. Continue buying unwaveringly when the market is up...or down. Just set it up to automatically debit out every month.

How much money do you need to retire on? The conventional wisdom is **25 times your annual personal expenditure.** And only receiving income of 3% - 4% per year (or cashing in the equivalent amount).

For example, if you spend £3,000 per month, then you'd need a fund of £900,000. That may sound daunting, but don't forget the law of compounding interest — it's all about starting early and allowing the years to do their magic.

In addition, if you can open the tracker in a tax-efficient wrapper (like an ISA in the UK), then you can receive tax free earnings…for life.

I'd also like to suggest bonds. My father invested in them.

Speak to an Independent Financial Adviser before you make an investing decision.

3) INTELLECTUAL PROPERTY (IP) & CONTENT CREATION

People usually think of more challenging ideas such as writing hit songs, creating a patent or selling franchise licenses.

However, we live in the information age. **It has never been easier for you to become a content creator**.

You could write a book or design a course. Or you could create content and make money from advertisers – there are a many social media millionaires.

What are you passionate about?

What niche expertise do you have that not many others do?

4) OTHER ASSET CLASSES

You can invest in commodities like gold and silver, art, classic cars and collectable watches. However, they don't pay you an income. They only rise and fall according to market conditions.

Although they can be a good way to park some of your money, I don't see them as primary investment vehicles.

Many of the Millionaires had investments in tax-free savings such as ISAs and premium bonds. Although these were not a substantial part of their portfolio, and they were mostly used as cash reserves to be used in an emergency.

Another passive income stream we utilise is **lending money** to property developments as joint ventures. We keep this to a tight circle of our existing friends. **The risk is significantly higher** than simply renting out properties or investing in an index tracker, so I don't recommend it as your main source of income.

Plus, you won't receive a monthly income as developments generally pay back at the end. Thus, lending money should only be a small part of your portfolio, if any at all. I recommend not going above 10% of your portfolio.

We've also done it the other way, where people have invested with us for a generous guaranteed return, and we've used their money to build our property portfolio. We frequently do this.

Cash Flow Versus Capital Appreciation

In the property industry, you can to some extent choose to aim for more capital appreciation, or more cash flow.

For example, if you bought a residential property to rent out, then the capital appreciation would generally be higher in the South East than the North of England.

But…the cash flow received from a property in the South East would be a lower return on investment, versus the North.

So which is better?

Definitely, 100 per cent, **cash flow is better for property investing if your plan is to become financially free.**

That was a difficult lesson for me to learn over the years. Waiting for properties or stock and shares to rise in value, does not pay the bills in the meantime.

Once you focus on cash flow first, then **it doesn't matter to you if there is a market crash.** You're holding for the long-term, so the cash still keeps rolling in every month.

Of the Stealth Millionaires that were doing commercial to residential conversions to sell — they had already established their cash flow generating investment portfolio before they started developments.

I see a lot of people make the mistake of starting with developments first, and then not receiving any money for the next 2-3 years. They wonder why they are living on the breadline, as they hold out for that big score!

And yes, even that three month build you're planning could take three years. One investor I know found Roman remains the moment they broke ground, resulting in closing the site while they waited for archaeologists. It took another a year to get bank finance and withdraw their money, due to unforeseen difficulties. Anything can happen.

The Wonders of Compounded Growth

Let's imagine you put £10,000 in a stock market index tracker and it increases an average of 5% per year. Of course, you divided this up into a monthly amount to avoid trying to time the market.

By the end of year one it would be worth £10,500.

If you didn't withdraw any funds, then by year five, your pot would be £12,763.

By the end of year 10 it would be worth £16,289.

The more time it's given to grow, the bigger it becomes. That's the power of compounding growth!

In the UK, provided you don't have a government pension, or defined benefit pension, you can transfer the funds to a SIPP or SSAS pension and manage it yourself. Pensions can be a great way to compound your wealth. You can also pass on the funds from your SIPP or SSAS pension to your beneficiaries. Speak to your Independent Financial Advisor.

But, I offer some caution.

Don't put all of your investing money into your pension, unless you are about to reach retirement age. There is a balance. **You need to be able to live now**. If you create a passive income that you can spend now, then you can retire early.

Leverage

All of our Stealth Millionaires leveraged their assets. This is simply **using bank or private lending to purchase property.**

Linda and Brian had the lowest Loan To Value (LTV) in their property portfolio, as Brian was the oldest person, at 70 years old. Many of the others tended to have an average LTV of 50-70%.

But what if you don't want to take out a mortgage on an investment property? How much difference will it make anyway?

Let's look at two simplified examples.

Scenario 1:
You buy a house for £100,000 in cash and receive £500 cash flow per month, after all expenses. That's £6,000 income per year.

On average, **property doubles in value every 7-9 years**.

Let's round it to 10 years. So by the end of a decade, your property investment is now worth £200,000. **You've just gained £100,000** in capital appreciation. Not bad at all.

Scenario 2:
You put down **£100,000 cash as a deposit across 4 houses** and **apply for mortgages** at 75% Loan to Value. Your total portfolio has a value of £400,000. If we assume a 4% interest rate on your mortgage of £150,000, then it will cost you about £1,000 per month...so you'll be making a net £1,000 cash flow per month. **Double the income of scenario 1.**

It gets better...

...after 10 years, all four properties will have doubled in value. Your portfolio will now be worth £800,000. So, **you've gained £400,000**. That's four times the appreciation of scenario 1.

Of course, like all investments, the market can move up and down. These are just averages. Your home is at risk, etc...

Don't Gamble — De-risk instead

> "Rule No. 1: Never lose money.
> Rule No. 2: Never forget rule No. 1."
>
> —WARREN BUFFET
> BILLIONAIRE INVESTOR

Gambling
The majority of our Millionaires did not play the lottery. With the chance of winning at 1 in 300 million or worse — **it was too much like gambling** for them.

That's not unusual. In a study published in the Journal Gambling Studies[5] they discovered that **the lowest income group spent the most on lotteries**. Therefore, the next time you're thinking about buying a lottery ticket, **consider putting the money in your index fund instead!**

On the other hand, some of our Millionaires did have money in the UK's National Premium Bonds. This is a lottery with a difference — **you get to keep your capital**. You are entered into the draw each month (for

---

[5] Barnes GM, Welte JW, Tidwell MC, Hoffman JH. Gambling on the lottery: sociodemographic correlates across the lifespan. J Gambl Stud. 2011;27(4):575–586. doi:10.1007/s10899-010-9228-7

free) and your winnings are tax free. You can also buy them for your children.

None of the Stealth Millionaires did day trading on the stock market either — they felt that was **too risky.** We all preferred the certainty that came with being long-term investors.

De-Risking Investments

All of our Millionaires accepted that there was some risk in the properties invested in — they would likely be evaluated as people with a medium to high-risk profile.

However, **they all felt they had de-risked** the deals, **so to them it was not risky**. They felt it was "safe as houses."

They looked for **multiple exit strategies**.

For example, let's consider buying a property to use as a holiday let. You've also checked the demand for use as a Buy to Let, in case you decide to switch the property's usage later. And in both cases, you've evaluated the return on investment, and they meet your target returns. You've also bought the property below market value, so even if the market dips you have baked in some value and could sell it without making a loss.

They also **spread their funds across multiple investments**. They didn't put all their eggs into one basket.

For example, we prefer to **buy multiple cheaper properties with the same pot of funds**, rather than just buying one expensive property. Otherwise, when the single property is empty, you will have to fund a loss every month.

If you're investing in the **stock market,** you could **consider multiple providers**, in case one collapses like Lehman Brothers did. You might also consider different index funds.

All of our Millionaires **banked with multiple banking groups**. Generally, this was a current account and banks for each business — they typically banked with 3-6 groups. They were with different banks for two main reasons:

1. If a bank collapsed, like Northern Rock did, then you would still be able to access funds from your other banks.
2. You would have access to multiple lines of credit and lending.
3. The UK's Financial Services Compensation Scheme currently guarantees up to £85,000 of your money, per banking group. You need to spread your cash out.

Going against the grain provides opportunities

Reportedly **more millionaires are made during a recession.**

Many of the Stealth Millionaires I spoke to were **optimistic about the idea of a housing market crash — they saw it as a great opportunity to buy.**

Why? Because the cash flow from the rental properties would not go down…in fact it would probably increase due to lack of properties available for rent.

In addition, they would be able to **pick up properties at a much bigger discount**. Of course, you need to have cash reserves ready for this, or to have access to private lending from other investors.

But what about their portfolios devaluing? They were all investing for the long-term, so it didn't matter if they went down in value. The masses may panic and try to sell, before the market drops too low — don't do it! Remember, property doubles every 7-9 years on average, so they will go back up. And as you may recall earlier, our **main investing focus is on cash flow**, not capital appreciation. **This protects us from crashes**.

You can apply the same logic to the stock market. Buying when the market has had a couple of weeks consistently trending upwards after a black swan crash (not the bottom), is another potential way to make substantial gains. I've done that a few times in the past.

You may need to **go against the grain when it comes to your friends**. If your friends are not millionaires, they will try to convince you that it's not possible for you to become a millionaire through property or stocks and shares. Because "if you could, everyone would be doing it." That's exactly why you should be doing it.

According to Credit Suisse's Global Wealth Report in 2019, less than 5% of UK adults are millionaires, and just over 7% are millionaires in North America.

Do what Millionaires do, not what the masses do.

Get Rich Slow

Most Stealth Millionaires grew their investment portfolio over many years.

They didn't do get rich quick schemes. They preferred the certainty of knowing how much return they could expect from their investments each year.

Conversely many lower-income people that I've met are trying for the "one big win" that will change their life. And they're prepared to risk all of their money to do it.

Be Tax Efficient — It's Not What You Earn, It's What You Keep

In addition to keeping their personal expenses under control, Millionaires took a number of tax-efficient steps to **squeeze more out of the money they earned**.

Businesses
The rich pay less income tax than everyone else.

Is that fair? Absolutely, as it is available for anyone to do — you just need the knowledge and £12.

Firstly, **they all have a company**. That could be as simple as a company that holds rental properties. At the time of print, you could register the company yourself for only £12.

Most people don't realise that being a company owner in the UK, means **you pay less personal tax than if you were an employee**. So, we get to take home more of our pay than you do.

There are certain **tax efficient perks**, like working from home allowances, education and training, travel expenses, annual parties, gifts, and company cars that you can benefit from.

You should hire an Accountant and Tax Planner, to make sure you follow the correct accounting procedures and set up your companies in the most tax-efficient way. The Stealth Millionaires felt that their Accountant saved them more tax than they cost.

In addition, there is a little-known tax benefit on Commercial Property called **Capital Allowances**. You can offset this against income, **effectively earning tax free money.**

A couple of the Stealth Millionaires have earned so much in Capital Allowances that **they won't need to pay any personal tax for years.** However, they will still need to pay National Insurance.

Protect Your Assets

Set up a Company

All of the Stealth Millionaires **operated multiple companies** and took out public liability and professional indemnity insurance.

They didn't have lots of employees. They might have someone helping with the accounts, managing their properties, or use a virtual assistant, but that was it.

Putting your assets into a company with **limited liability** protects you in a number of ways.

If someone is attacking your personal assets, say, if you have given a personal guarantee or are being sued, then they can't touch the assets in any of your companies. It's another reason not to own the home you live in as you could lose that too.

Conversely, if you were to do a development and you bought it in a Special Purpose Vehicle (a company with only this property in it), then if it all goes completely wrong, **you will only lose the money you invested**.

Another common action they took, was **not to combine trading activities in companies with assets.** For example, if you have real estate in a company, but you get sued for your trading activities in that company (such as managing other people's properties), then you might end up having your real estate liquidated and lose all of it. Conversely if your property management was in a company of its own, then they can't touch your real estate.

Accountants tend to want you to link all the companies together, with one company receiving all the income at the top.

But most of the Millionaires kept the companies completely separate, so that if one went down it wouldn't affect any of the others.

One of my Millionaire friends Paul goes one step further — he puts his employees in a separate company and then charges their time to his other companies. That way, if any employee takes legal action on his staff company, it doesn't kill his income or assets.

Inheritance Tax & Trusts

The advantage of a trust is that it sits outside of your estate, so it is a good way to reduce Inheritance Tax. Again, **a trust is a separate entity from you, so it provides protection**.

The use of a Trust reportedly enabled the late Duke of Westminster to pass on the majority of his **£8.3 billion estate with no death duties to pay!** A large proportion of the investments were in real estate, and included property in the upmarket areas of Belgravia and Mayfair in London.

All of the Millionaires had a pension. You can pay into this tax-free, up to certain amounts each year. All the earnings are tax-free whilst they are in the pension. **Many had transferred their personal pension into a SSAS pension**, so they could take control of what the pension fund invested in. In particular they used it for investing in Commercial Property or developments.

A SSAS pension is set up under a Trust. It can have multiple members, such as your adult children.

Wills

Research by Royal London found that **54% of people in the UK did not have a will**.[6] Perhaps more alarming is that 59% of parents did not have a will — so if the worst happened, then their children might not go to the person they hoped for. **All of the Stealth Millionaires had a will.**

People don't realise that **wills are a great tax planning tool**. For example, if you have your parents in the will and you die before them, then effectively the funds from your estate could get taxed twice. Once upon your death, and once upon theirs.

Keep your will up to date. If you have an **ex husband or wife** and they are still in your will, then **they will gain access to your money**…and can decide what to do with your body.

---

[6] Perplexed by wills: more than 5 million adults do not know where to begin. Royal London, 5 December 2018

Chapter Four Summary:
Invest

- Become recession-proof with multiple streams of income — you need at least three legs on your stool
- Buy properties
  - Leverage property with mortgages and lending for greater profits
  - Prioritise real estate cash flow over capital appreciation
- Don't gamble — de-risk instead
  - Don't do "get rich quick" schemes. Get rich slow. Re-invest to compound your wealth over many years
  - Don't buy lottery tickets
  - Don't day trade — you can't play poker against the best players on earth.
- Invest in a low-cost index tracking fund
- Create Intellectual Property
- You can take control of your pension investments in a SIPP or SSAS
- Going against the grain can provide opportunities
- Be tax efficient — it's what you keep that matters. Start a business, use trusts, keep your will up-to-date and use tax-free investments
- Protect your assets! Use multiple companies, trusts, wills, and professional and public liability insurance

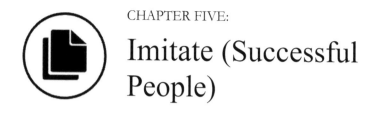

CHAPTER FIVE:

Imitate (Successful People)

Modelling

Humans naturally model each other. Consider children, learning to walk, to speak, and to feed themselves. Kids will copy both your good and bad habits.

> "If you're not growing, you're dying."
>
> —TONY ROBBINS

Tony Robbins recommends you pick one person who is successful or has created the life you want to live — then copy them. There's no need to reinvent the wheel.

What steps did they take?

What are their attitudes and habits?

What challenges came up?

What sacrifices did they need to make?

How can we think like them?

Modelling is one of main the steps Sarah and I took, to learn how to become Financially Free. We researched people who had achieved it, to see what made them tick. What did they do, that the masses did not?

Our learnings are summarised in this book and our #1 bestselling book ***RETIRE NOW! Your Blueprint to Financial Freedom Through Property***. mycastleproperty.co.uk/books

Nearly all of **our Stealth Millionaires admired a number of people with success in different arenas**. There were many examples across business, particular property strategies, mindset, and health and fitness.

They didn't want to be them. They were interested in certain skills, where those people had excelled. They were also interested in how they structured their businesses.

Andrew took this one stage further. He didn't only look at famous people at the top of their game. He regularly looked for specific skills or traits to admire in people within his own network that were slightly ahead of, or behind him.

None of the Stealth Millionaires resented successful people. All of them saw successful people as opportunities to learn and grow.

Admiring successful people can be a difficult change in mindset for some. It can bring out jealousy and some of the worst behaviour.

Money and power can make you more of what you already are – it doesn't change you. If you are a good person, then more money enables you to do more good in the world.

If you're struggling with admiration, then become self-aware and try to find people to model who share some of your values.

How to Learn From Them?

There are so many opportunities to learn. Nearly all of our Stealth Millionaires spent a lot of money every year to learn how to become more successful in their business, and personal life. **They prioritise learning above most other wants**.

Most experts have free content in the form of a regular blog, podcast or video. This is a great way to get to know them and see whether you like what you're hearing.

From there, you can progress to a low-cost information item, such as a book or video series.

After that, it's usually paid courses, masterminds, or mentoring programmes.

Many people think paying for courses is a waste of money.

However, the majority of our **Stealth Millionaires regularly paid tens of thousands of pounds for courses and had paid for a mentor** in the past. This was despite most of them being mentors themselves — there is always the opportunity to learn more.

A mentor can compress decades of learning into days. The Stealth Millionaires preferred to save years of mistakes by learning from people who'd achieved the result already.

In addition to the paid mentoring, most of the Millionaires regularly participated in masterminds. They were all avid book readers.

Build your Network

"I learned that it pays to hang around with people better than you are, because you will float upward a little bit.

And if you hang around with people that behave worse than you, pretty soon you'll start sliding down the pole.

It just works that way

−WARREN BUFFET
BILLIONAIRE INVESTOR

You may have heard the adage "Your network is your net worth."

Despite how confident I appear speaking on stage, or when being filmed, I'm naturally an introverted person.

I recharge after a long day, by being with my family, or alone. If I went to a nightclub, I'd be the one hiding in the corner wondering how to strike up a conversation with strangers. Consequently, I have always disliked going to networking meetings.

Sarah is completely the opposite. She can easily strike up a conversation with a random person, whilst standing in a queue at the supermarket. My nine-year-old son is the same as Sarah.

What took me many years to realise, is that "networking" by meeting hundreds of people in an evening is not important. The value is gained from the number of hours you spend with a small group of people each month.

A couple of years ago we took a long, hard look at who we spent our time with, outside of our family.

We made intentional steps to spend more hours with millionaire property investors, and less time with everyone else. These are all strong relationships. We have each other's backs, and call upon each other for advice. It's a two-way street.

Most of the Stealth Millionaires spent a larger proportion of their time with other millionaire friends, rather than people from their "old life". Although, Sarah and I were the only people who constructed this intentionally.

Having a strong network is invaluable.

If you tell your poor friends you want to become a millionaire, they will laugh at you.

If you tell your millionaire friends, they will ask you how you plan to do it and will support you.

What kind of topics will your poor friends be discussing? How they hate their jobs? How they read about some celebrity doing this or that?

How would that compare with your millionaire friends?

They'd be talking about the great investment they'd just made, the tax they had saved, or how a negative change in regulations could lead to an opportunity if you did the opposite of the masses.

And you'd be able to ask your millionaire friends questions, so you can learn to do it too.

Subscribe to our weekly Financial Freedom and Property Investing video newsletter at: mycastleproperty.co.uk/joinus

Chapter Five Summary:
Imitate (Admire and Model Successful People)

- Don't resent successful people — admire and model their habits
- Invest in your education — read, watch videos, listen to podcasts, take courses, get a mentor who's achieved what you desire
- Build your network — quality hours, not number of contacts
- Spend more of your time with millionaire friends and learn from them

IMAGINE EARNING YOUR FIRST MILLION...

Close your eyes and think about it.

What will you life look like?

What kind of house will you live in?

How will you spend your days with your loved ones?

Which far off countries will you travel to?

But...you're wondering what steps do you need to take to make your new life a reality?

We completely replaced our incomes when Sarah was only 39 years old and have a property portfolio worth £2 million.

We can show you exactly how we did it, by taking you step-by-step through what it takes to become completely Financially Free.

We can help you to create an action plan, and support you carrying it out — so you never need to worry about money again.

To Achieve your Dream Life faster, visit
mycastleproperty.co.uk/training

CHAPTER SIX:

Millionaire Mindset

George's Family Upbringing

My father grew up in Hong Kong. He was looking forward to his first day of school, at the age of five, on 8th December 1941.

Instead, he awoke to the frightening noise of explosions, as the Japanese bombed Kai Tak Airport. And so began Japan's occupation of Hong Kong, during World War II.

School was cancelled. He had to educate himself now.

He lived a life of survival. At age five, he learned how to cook for himself, and take care of himself. He would often be left all alone, because his father had gone to war, and his mother was at a sewing factory…so he had no choice.

When he ran out of food, he would visit the Japanese prisoner of war camps and beg for scraps.

*****

I grew up in a modest three-bedroom house on a council estate. We didn't have a lot of money in the early years of my childhood. I remember envying other children who had the latest toys.

My father was extremely self-sufficient. He grew much of his own food. I have lots of fond memories of collecting and eating fruit off the trees and bushes in our garden. There were glass demijohn under the kitchen table, fermenting wine.

He made his secret recipe of lethal chilli paste. He cooked all food from fresh ingredients, as he hated packaged foods. He cut our hair. He serviced his car on his own. He laid his own patio and built brick outbuildings in the garden.

He laboured for everything and disliked the idea of paying someone else. If anything broke, he tried to fix it. And when it broke again, he would continue repairing it until at last…it fell apart.

My father worked in the operating theatres of our local hospital. It was a very modest salary, around the national average.

What I didn't realise at the time, was that he spent most of his spare income paying off the mortgage on our home…as fast as possible. He made over-payments. And he invested in the stock market at the same time.

He was a small business entrepreneur. I saw him do painting and decorating at weekends. Later, he set up a

business cooking Chinese food for dinner parties in people's homes.
My mother didn't work, as she needed to look after me. So, he bought her an ice cream van. I was less than six years old at the time.

I remember turning on the Greensleeves tune in the van to announce we'd arrived in each street. Children and adults would come out of their houses with excitement. I'd then help to sell the ice cream, sweets, and cigarettes.

This was my early taste of running a home business, or having a "side hustle".

There seemed to be more income available in the years after my sister was born, when my mother could hold down a full-time job. Whilst my father was extremely tight with his money, my mother spent everything that was in her bank account. She would spoil my sister and me with presents.

This was a dichotomy. In order to live within our means, my father took responsibility for paying all the bills and investing. He deposited money into a separate bank account for my mother, to ringfence her spending.

The years that followed were a massive spending spree for me. I followed my mother's example. I spent money on things that didn't matter.

Looking back, I can see that I chased labels and other symbols of success. I enjoyed the thrill of paying a large amount of money in a shop. **I wanted to prove to the world that I was a higher social status** — that I wasn't poor.

I never budgeted. I always ran out of money...I racked up debt on my credit card.

It was only when I finally moved out of the family home, and Sarah and I rented an apartment, that I finally grew up and took responsibility. I wasn't going to be bailed out anymore. It was stupid to have bad debt. I needed to live within my means.

We decided to get joint bank accounts and have always operated as a single unit since then. We're like the Borg from Star Trek! We have collective thoughts and spend as one hive.

One pay rise led to another. Although I'd curbed most of my spend and had invested in the stock market and real estate, I was still seeking status symbols. Still trying to prove myself.

The dramatic change came when Sarah and I decided we wanted to become Financially Free. We didn't want to keep working until we were 65 years old. We wanted to live our lives.

I said to myself. If I had a **gun pointed at my head and had to retire within the next six months**, how would I do it?

And so began our research into other people that had achieved it.

How were they able to retire so young?

What habits should we be modelling?

Those Millionaire habits are in this book.

The way we built our property empire is in our book *RETIRE NOW! Your Blueprint to Financial Freedom Through Property.*
mycastleproperty.co.uk/books

Sarah's Family Upbringing

Her father was part of a farming family. They had four kids and were relatively affluent at the time. He grew up in a nice house with lots of land. He was relatively thrifty, and had practical skills.

Sarah's mother came from a poorer background. She lived in a council house. She was extremely thrifty with her money.

Both of her parents were good at living within their means and also accounting. They were always saving and tracking their spending.

Sarah and her sister got socks for birthday presents. The only frivolous presents were from grandparents. Sarah would go shopping with one of her grandparents, once a week — who would buy her a bag of sweets and a small toy. Apart from that, they only received gifts at Christmas and birthdays.

Sarah's mother used to help Sarah enter competitions, and she won some toys that way. Despite this, Sarah didn't feel hard done by growing up.

Her parents were both quite entrepreneurial — they often had two or three small businesses running at the same time. Sarah's mum mostly worked during school hours — although she sometimes dragged Sarah and her sister along with her.

At sixteen, Sarah worked in a factory to save for University. She put the money in a bank account and didn't spend any of it.

At University, her parents gave her £20 a week for food, and Sarah paid for everything else out of her savings. She managed to come out of Uni with no debt, apart from a student loan that she had taken out to invest.

When she met me, I was still over-spending. Some of her budgeting skills rubbed off on me, and she helped me to get out of debt.

We lived within our means when we moved in together, but I also rubbed off on her. We spent more on designer clothes and cars than she was used to — we even bought tailored suits. We were only in our twenties at the time.

As we got older and thought about the future, we started to treat our personal expenses more like a business. We spent less on stuff that wasn't important and did more tracking and planning.

Once we started investing in property, we became far more motivated to save than spend. After a while, it became addictive! Particularly when we didn't need to work full time anymore…and then when we became totally Financially Free.

We've had such a massive mind shift. "Bizarrely when I speak to my parents," Sarah said, "I've come back full circle to the more sensible spending habits I had as a child."

"It's a shame I didn't maintain that when I was a young adult. Because had we done that, **we would have been Financially Free in our twenties**."

Watch out for Negative Verbal Programming

If you're bad with money and not rich yet, the chances are **you've been programmed to think negatively about money**.

Your wealth thermostat is set at a specific level, and whenever you receive a windfall of money you blow it to make sure you are back to your usual temperature.

This negative programming will keep you poor, until you can recognise it, and **change your language and behaviour**.

One lady I spoke to told me "Money is a broken promise." When she was a child, her father would promise holidays and various gifts, but they never happened. This led to her spending most of her life giving away all her money to family and charity, because she wanted to make sure she was delivering on her promises to other people — but at a detriment to her financial stability.

Have a think about yourself. Are there any **negative statements you learned as a child** which you strongly believe in?

"Money doesn't grow on trees."

"We can't afford it."

"Rich people are a**holes."

"Rich people are greedy."

"Money can't buy you happiness."

"Money is the root of all evil."

"Money isn't important."

"I want, doesn't get."

The first two statements are ones that I grew up with. Even today…being a millionaire, Financially Free and never needing to work again, I still find myself saying to my children "We can't afford it."

This is usually because they've suggested wasting money on a £300 lifelike baby doll — yes, you really can spend that much! Or my son wants us to buy a new car, such as a Ferrari or Lamborghini.

I catch myself saying "We can't afford it." Then **I try to remember to reframe** and restate it again. **"We CAN afford it!** But I'd rather invest the money instead."

"Money doesn't grow on trees?" There's plenty of money around. You will have more if you invest it and re-invest the returns for compounded growth. Remember, **every pound is a seedling**. You can **re-invest your seedlings to grow a forest.**

But, there must be some joy in spending the income generated by your assets. So, where possible, **try to link statements to fun**, such as enabling you to go on holiday instead.

Consequently, the next time you hear yourself **saying something negative about money, take a breath and reframe it.** Here's another question…

Is money important to you?

If you answered "no," then you have a problem.

If you'd rather give than make money…or spend than make money…then you have a poor mindset. **You will always be poor** unless you make it important.

You must be willing to become a money magnet and believe that <u>money is important</u> to you.

If you find it hard to accept the above statement, because you want to give everything to charity, then consider this…

- The Bill & Melinda Gates Foundation have spent over $53.8 billion on charitable programmes over the last 20 years
- Warren Buffet donated $3.6 billion in stock to the Bill & Melinda Gates Foundation in 2019
- Amazon's Jeff Bezos donated $100 million to the food bank charity Feeding America in 2020
- Tony Robbins, in partnership with Feeding America, provided over 525 million meals over 5 years

These are only a couple of examples of the many considerable donations made to charity every year.

If you want to do more for charity, then aim not to exceed 10% in donations…so the more profitable you can make your businesses, the more money you can give away to charity.

All of the wealthy people we know have some form of "giving back". Be it volunteering, giving to charity or helping people.

Whilst I am sure that there are many wealthy a**holes out there – you don't have to be one of them. It shouldn't prevent you from accumulating wealth, as you can make more of a difference to people when you are rich yourself – rather than needing the help.

Your Wealth Set Point

I strongly believe that everyone has a wealth set point and it is stopping them from becoming rich.

Imagine a **wealth thermostat**. It is set at £10,000 in savings.

You get a big bonus at work. Suddenly **your monkey mind freaks out**. It's getting too hot to handle the extra cash…

So you blow it. A new TV that you didn't need, a party for your friends, another holiday, a new car for the one that you weren't planning to replace yet.

Phew, you've got back to your comfortable level of savings again…

…and you never seem to save any more money.

Tell your mind **"you are a great receiver of money."** Set your wealth thermostat higher.

Money is a Tool. Money is Abundant.

Poor people want money, for money's sake. However, **Stealth Millionaires viewed money as an enabler.** It enables you to do what you want, both for yourself and others.

We don't have the stress of working anymore and enjoy having our days out and trips to the spa when our kids are at school. We also mentor people a couple of days per month, to have a purpose by transforming people's lives.

You may not think it, but **money is abundant**. Money used to be a "Gold Standard." Paper money could be converted into a fixed amount of gold. However, that was later abandoned for the "Fiat System," where the government decrees it must be accepted for payment.

Quantitative Easing is used by many governments to keep inflation low and stable. The central banks like Bank of England and U.S. Federal Reserve **print money out of thin air** (or rather electronically) and uses it to buy assets such as government bonds from pension funds.

According to the Bank of England, they purchased £435 billion of government bonds in 2019, and £645 billion in March 2020.

Money doesn't just disappear when you spend it. Imagine you take your family for a meal at a restaurant. The restaurant takes that money and uses it towards staff wages. One of the staff uses it to put petrol in their car. The owner of the petrol station uses it to buy his weekly groceries, and so on…money just keeps on circulating around. It doesn't disappear.

According to the Bank of England, the bank notes in circulation during 2019 were worth £71 billion. **Money is abundant.**

If you have a profitable deal to invest in, there will be someone willing to lend you the money.

Take Responsibility for Your Life

Are you, or do you know someone whose life is a disaster? They seem to be a **crap magnet**. Everything goes wrong. They crash their car, their relationships go bad, people are always against them, they lend people money who don't pay them back...

> "You must take personal responsibility. You cannot change the circumstances, the seasons, or the wind, but you can change yourself."
>
> —JIM ROHN

It may be a bitter pill for them to swallow, but the reason they are a crap magnet, is because they have a victim mentality.

The **Law of Attraction brings into our life whatever we focus on** — whether positive or negative.

Thus, if you are constantly thinking about how everyone is against you, and how you've been hard done by, then **you will continue to be a crap magnet** and drag everyone down with you.

Conversely, if you want to transform your life, you should start recognising positivity and opportunities. Every time you hear yourself talking like a victim…stop and start a new conversation about what is good in your life.

Gratitude
A **useful tool** we use as a family is **a *Gratitude Diary*.** A two-week study of people filling out their Gratitude Diary each day, concluded that the diary "effectively decreased depression, negative thinking and hopelessness and increased gratitude."[7]

Our Gratitude Diary is nothing fancy — it's just a notepad by my bed. Every evening, before we put our children to bed, I write down **up to three things I am grateful for** that day. I then ask Sarah and my kids what they're thankful for.

If you are having a really bad day, then it could be as simple as "I'm alive." Or sunshine. Or wine. If you're not even grateful for those and can't think of anything at all, then go back and read all the things you were grateful for.

---

[7] Leyland, Moray. (2012). Gratitude diaries as part of the CBT toolkit: Do they ameliorate depression, negative thinking and hopelessness, and increase gratitude?.

You can increase the positive effect of the Gratitude Diary by spending five minutes connecting with the emotions of those three things you were grateful for.

You Have More Control

The philosophy of **stoicism teaches us how to have a happy life.**

You don't need to worry about everything. **You have a lot more control over your life than you think.**

The *Dichotomy of Control* tells us what we should concern ourselves about.

If it is something over which we have no control whatsoever, such as the sun rising in the morning, a recession, or pandemic, then we should not spend time worrying about that issue. Instead, look at what you can control.

If we have complete control, such as whether we exercised, ate healthy food, saved money, bought stocks and shares, or purchased an investment property, then those are things within our control. We should focus on them. These are great options for goals.

However, there are some things where we only have partial control or influence in the outcome. So, look at what you can control in those situations.

Attraction with Action — Goal Setting

> "Do. Or do not.
> There is no try."
>
> —MASTER YODA
> STAR WARS EPISODE V

Whilst I believe in the *Law of Attraction* to an extent, I don't feel you can just wish it to happen.

None of the Stealth Millionaires just wished for things using the Law of Attraction. All of them were action takers. **There was always a plan** to achieve what they wanted. They were all doers.

Joy said, "The Law of Attraction takes work, not wishing."

On the wall of our home office we have what we like to call a *Dream Board*.

A **Dream Board is a single page, containing what we want to Have, Be, or Do in our life**. These are both short-term and lifetime goals. We focus more on Be and Do as those will create more happiness for you than buying stuff.

It's great to create a combined dream board with your partner, to make sure you know where you are heading.

You can't achieve your goal without action. If becoming a Millionaire is a goal on your Dream Board, then you need to have a separate goals sheet breaking that down into actions. What are you going to do to achieve it. **Actions and habits make things happen.**

Sarah and I review our business performance and Dream Board every month. We also plan the top five priorities for the week together.

If we have specific habits, then we usually put them in our diary and tick them off as we do them — such as exercising and daily meditation.

Live Your Dreams

The Dream Board helps you to make your dreams a reality.

All of our Stealth Millionaires knew what their core values were. Consequently, these were the things they spent the most time, money and enjoyment on.

If you want a mansion you can buy it.

If you want a Rolex or Cartier watch, you can buy it.

If you want a Ferrari, Lamborghini or Aston Martin, you can buy it.

You can buy whatever you want.

However, to a large extent, the Stealth Millionaires had all de-linked the need to show off their status — they were off the Hedonic Treadmill. They had **achieved a mindset change that the public herd will not achieve**. They were not swayed so much by the propaganda techniques encouraging the masses to consume.

This enabled them to spend their life doing **what they wanted**, with the people that mattered most.

My father wanted to visit his home country of Hong Kong one last time. He was sick. He had type II diabetes and Parkinson's. Every year he delayed the trip "until he got better."

He had the money. But every year, he got worse.

It got to the point where he was like a vegetable. He couldn't sit in a chair without being strapped to it — otherwise he slid to the floor.

My father kept getting sicker. I sat beside his hospital bed for a depressing two weeks, as he slipped in and out of consciousness. He passed away, having never taken his last dream trip.

Sarah and I are very good at out of the box thinking. We frequently ask people to identify their values and dreams, and write them on their dream board. Quite often we ask "why are you not doing these things already?"

They shrug.

"Not enough money."

"Could you get paid to do it? Or get it for free instead?"

A look of puzzlement crosses their face.

One nurse said she wanted to work for Doctors without Borders — at some point, when she could afford it.

She was single. Her children were grown up. She owned her home.

She could receive a salary from Doctors without Borders. Why didn't she rent out her home? She hadn't realised…she didn't need to wait, to live her dreams.

Money is not the end game. Living is.

Look deep inside yourself. **Find out what is really important to you. Then Live Your Dreams.**

Be Willing to Fail — but Fail Small

At school, we become averse to failure. It stops us from taking risks. However, to grow your wealth, there will be risks.

During your journey to become a Millionaire, **you will make many mistakes.** Maybe like us, you bought at the peak of house prices, just before a crash.

Just accept these outcomes and learn what you could do better in future. You can't control a crash, but you could build in as much value into the property before hand, and make sure the cash flow stacks up.

One of my friends Jonathan, who is nearly a billionaire, gave me a great piece of advice:

"Don't do the deal that kills you."

One of the ways to make sure failures small, is to not put all your eggs in one basket. If you're buying properties, then split your funds as deposits on lots of cheaper properties.

That way, if something goes wrong with one, or you lose all your money on an investment, then you still have the others providing you with cash flow.

Chapter Six Summary:
Millionaire Mindset

- It is possible to turn yourself from a credit card spending shopaholic, into a saver and investor. George did it
- Watch out for negative verbal programming given to you as a child, such as "Money doesn't grow on trees." Reframe your thoughts and change what you say to others
- The goal is not to get "money." Money is only a tool to enable what you want. Focus on that instead
- Money is abundant — if you have a great deal, someone will lend you the money
- Take responsibility for your life
- Don't be a crap magnet
- For a happy life — focus on gratitude and what you can control
- Set your goals AND the actions to achieve them
- Spread your cash across multiple investments, and fail small
- Don't do the deal that kills you
- Remember to Live Your Dreams!

CHAPTER SEVEN:

Offspring (Don't Ruin Your Kids)

Don't Give Them a Free Ride

We have two children, aged 9 and 10. We think a lot about the effect we have on our children, as we've seen others go off the rails.

I've seen the son of a multi-millionaire throw their life away. He was given a house, car and money. This made him completely unmotivated to achieve anything in life…and turned him into an alcoholic and drug user.

I've seen another with little care about racking up bad debt, because he was just waiting for the day he would get his inheritance.

Usually **the "weakest" child gets all the financial support**…and yet, that **makes them even weaker**.

Those parents are still having to support their children, when they become grandparents. We don't want that for ourselves.

My parents paid for all my living costs whilst I was at university. Conversely, Sarah worked and saved up a pot of money to cover her living costs. Who do you think budgeted better as a student?

I was terrible, always going over my budget each term. I only started managing my money when I left home and had to support myself.

Sarah and I hope that we can enable our children to become motivated, financially self-sufficient and unentitled.

First generation rich kids had to graft and struggle to become Millionaires. In the early days we gave up our weekends and evenings to get our property portfolio started. We're so glad we did, as it taught us to be responsible.

I'm **not going to hand my children cash to buy houses.** But, **we are planning to lend money** to our children at a favourable interest rate in the early days, rather than give them money. Many of the Stealth Millionaires with adult children have already done this.

However, we want them to feel the pain of saving for their first house, without any financial help from us. These are money management skills for life.

We may give money to our children as part of a tax-saving gifting strategy, when they (and we) are much older, and they have built up a substantial investment portfolio on their own.

Education — Only If You Can Afford the Extras

I don't count education as spoiling them…providing you're not covering their expense account!

There are many benefits of sending your kids to private school, such as smaller class sizes, better facilities, and meeting a network of affluent people.

Richard was the only Stealth Millionaire to go to private school.

Sarah and I did go to university, but we did not go to private schools. Neither had any of the Stealth Millionaire's children…so far.

Sarah and I don't plan to send our children to private school. However, if they really want to go to university because they are passionate about it, then we will let them — but we won't encourage it.

Given what we know about how to become a Millionaire, then **going to the right school or university, has little impact on whether you will become a self-made Millionaire**.

That's an interesting statement, given that many of our Millionaires had gone to university. However, what's become clear to us is that the education system creates workers, not business owners. Consider the business owners who dropped out of university, like Bill Gates, Steve Jobs and Mark Zuckerberg.

Then you have those that never went to university, like Tony Robbins, Lord Sugar and Sir Richard Branson.

Moreover, there are hidden costs of private education, such as uniforms, sports gear and expensive class holidays. There's also conspicuous consumption. How will your child feel about being dropped off in a Hyundai, at a car park of full Range Rovers, Bentleys and G wagons?

I know a number of single mothers who feel they have to sacrifice more for their children, to cover the guilt they are feeling from a failed marriage. The children were used to a higher standard of living when they had a father living with them, and the mothers don't want to take that from them. They want to give everything.

They are willing to take themselves (and their family) close to bankruptcy, just to pay the fees for their children at the private school. It seems crazy to me to lead such a stressful life.

Instead they could invest those school fees in the stock market, or as a deposit on at least one property per year, giving cash flow for life. Wouldn't that provide a better life for their children? And there would be a legacy to pass onto them.

Should You Encourage Entrepreneurship or a Profession?

We plan to have our children start their own property business. Richard feels the same.

Linda and Brian, Joy and Andrew, all have grown up children. Interestingly, despite them all having their own businesses, they've just allowed their children to follow whatever career they wanted. Only Linda and Brian's children were property investors, at the time of writing this book.

Whilst it would be fantastic if my kids were interested in a property related profession, Sarah and I plan to **encourage our children to follow the profession they are passionate about**, so they can excel. And then invest their money in property or the stock market.

In addition, we don't want to hire them to work for us full time. I'm sure, like Sarah and me, you've had your fair share of bad managers. We'd much rather our children get a job with someone else. After a while, they will hopefully realise it's much better being your own boss.

Chapter Seven Summary:
Don't Ruin Your Kids

- Don't give them a free ride — they become unmotivated and can't manage their money
- Lend your children money in return for an interest rate, instead of giving it to them
- You don't need to go to a private school or university to become a Millionaire
- Only pay for education if you really can afford it without affecting your Financial Freedom — be aware of the hidden extras.
- Allow your children to follow their passions — but teach them how to invest and manage their money

FINAL THOUGHTS:

Go Forth and Become a Stealth Millionaire

To recap, these are the **seven habits** to becoming a Stealth Millionaire:

We began this book to discover whether there were any learnable habits that could make you a Millionaire. We were not disappointed.

It was interesting to note that all of our Stealth Millionaires thought they were unique and did things that others would not.

Whilst that may be true for the masses, that was not the case for Millionaires. **We all had very similar habits**.

Becoming a self-made Millionaire will require sacrifice. You will need to sacrifice time and money — saving, not spending.

The people with the most flash lifestyles, are often the poorest. They have nothing left at the end of the month. Is it worth limping along at work for the next 40 years, because you refuse to temporarily downgrade your living standard?

Or would you rather save 50-75% of your income and retire within five years or less? Then you can upgrade your lifestyle.

Compound interest is your biggest friend. Millionaires get rich over time. They don't do get rich quick schemes.

They are **cautious about upgrading their lifestyles** too much. They live within their means and save every single month.

They enjoy spending on what is most important to them — whether that's on their home, holidays, luxury cars, personal development, or having fun days out. Their assets pay for their spending.

Stealth Millionaires get to wear whatever they want. **They don't need to impress anyone** to prove their status. They've already made it.

Anyone can learn the spending, saving and investing habits outlined in this book. It doesn't matter what social class you are…what job you have…or which school you went to.

Get ready to become the next Stealth Millionaire.

George & Sarah Choy

We can help you to create an action plan, and support you carrying it out — so you never need to worry about money again.

To Achieve your Dream Life faster, visit
mycastleproperty.co.uk/training

IMAGINE EARNING YOUR FIRST MILLION...

Close your eyes and think about it.

What will you life look like?

What kind of house will you live in?

How will you spend your days with your loved ones?

Which far off countries will you travel to?

But...you're wondering what steps do you need to take to make your new life a reality?

We completely replaced our incomes when Sarah was only 39 years old and have a property portfolio worth £2 million.

We can show you exactly how we did it, by taking you step-by-step through what it takes to become completely Financially Free.

We can help you to create an action plan, and support you carrying it out — so you never need to worry about money again.

To Achieve your Dream Life faster, visit
mycastleproperty.co.uk/training

Other Books by the Authors

RETIRE NOW! Your Blueprint to Financial Freedom Through Property

"This is a very useful read for those wanting a no-nonsense approach to achieving financial freedom (warts and all)."

Raj Beri
Your Property Network (YPN) Magazine

"If you are serious about creating wealth, this book will give you a very solid foundation"

Kevin Whelan
Founder of WealthBuilders

"They have a unique approach of attempting to only work one hour a month on their property business… This book has the power to transform lives."

Paul Smith
Touchstone Education

**Buy RETIRE NOW today:
mycastleproperty.co.uk/books**

Printed in Great Britain
by Amazon